Apostasy of the Earthmen

צמח בן אלון

(Tzemach Ben Alon)

Prologue

Prophecies tell us that before the end of time we will be sent a prophet to warn us of the coming dangers. Biblical students are already advising that signs of the end times are happening every day but there have been so many predictions of the end of the world that never happened nobody now believes.

The problem that would face a prophet or messenger today is the apostasy of the inhabitants of the Earth. In a time where anti-religious and wealthy elites control the narrative the messenger would be silenced. Media and social media are controlled to such an extent that the elite and powerful overlords can spread any lies or accusations with impunity. They distort facts and present their narrative as the truth and even when reporting news, they can announce it such a way as to affect the perception to one of their own liking.

The Bible is almost never read and by and large is no longer given any credence. Biblical works are regularly treated with derision regarded as something of a joke only because very few really know anything about the contents of the Bible and fewer know the context.

The amount of ignorance and misunderstanding about what is in the Bible probably means that should the prophet appear nobody would have a clue what he was talking about and he would stand a good chance of being locked up as being mentally unstable, if he tried to teach

Biblical law on social media he would be banned for spreading hate speech. If the Almighty appeared and spoke to you how could you ever tell anyone without being considered delusional?

Zechariah 3:8 ... behold I bring forth my servant the branch

Malachi 4:5 Behold I will send you Elijah the prophet before the coming of the great and dreadful day of the Lord.

Chapter 1

"Religion is the cause of all the world's problems; it is a fairy story with no merit." The belligerent tone announced the attitude of a militant atheist the worst type of zealot. The atheist is convinced that because in his mind any type of supreme being is an impossibility he believes that he is the pinnacle of creation or evolution. To refer to his belief system as his religion is enough to elicit a violent response and at the very least abuse.

"Do you really believe that? Have you thought it through?" I asked, he responded, "Why; do you think I am wrong?" I felt I had to inform him, "Religion is an intangible it is an idea, a belief, a paradigm it doesn't do anything. It is the belief and behaviour of men that does all the damage. The requirements of the Judeo/Christian belief is that we should love God and act with righteousness, justice, kindness, and mercy. Religion did not teach men to burn their fellow man at the stake for belonging to another religion. Only one religion urges followers to harass or kill non-believers.

The basis of the major religions is the Bible and any teaching that goes against the Biblical law is obviously not really religious, but man made." The argument seemed to stall with this as the accuser paused in thought. It was apparent that such a simple philosophy or argument was not going to carry the day. In his closed mind religion was still evil and false not to be trusted; the closed mind of the atheist could not comprehend it because he knows so little of what constitutes religion and faith.

"If God is real why does he allow famines and wars to kill so many people?" "God does not allow these things they are caused by men who do not know God or the Bible. If everyone followed the Biblical teaching, there would be no wars and we could produce enough food in areas of plenty to take care of people who live in lands where there is famine. Before you ask why does God not do something, ask what have you done or what could you do to help. We are not here to be spectators we should work to improve the world and the lot of our fellow man.

Many years ago, my Mother would say to me, "God did not put you on this Earth for decoration, you should strive to leave it a better place for you having been here." I would tease her by saying, "He could have put me here for decoration I am good looking enough." Alas now that I have lived many years my youthful good looks have evaporated and I now realise that although I have done many good things there are many more things I could have done had I made a greater effort. I am afraid that is the case with many people, except that many others do no good works and others make the situation worse due to greed or dishonesty and the mistreatment of others."

Apostasy of the Earthmen

What is religion that it causes such dissension? Surveys show that two thirds of society know little of religion and because they do not know it think it unbelievable and impossible. Western society was originally founded on Judeo/Christian concepts that evolved initially from the Ten Commandments. There are six hundred and thirteen commandments in the Bible. Two hundred and forty-eight saying "thou shall" and three hundred and sixty-five "thou shall not" but ten were deemed so important that they were given directly by the hand of the Almighty.

Western society developed all their laws from the Biblical instructions but in recent decades many have worked hard to replace them with laws of their own invention, or more accurately developed by a vocal minority. The acceptance of homo sexuality as a life choice is a prime example but society has also become more accepting of adultery, promiscuity, incest (in some jurisdictions if participants are adult) and other sexual immorality. The new morality is still not accepting of bestiality but only on the grounds of animal cruelty.

Along with the moral decay has come a loss of the work ethic and an expectation that reward will follow effort. Much of this is part of the communist manifesto which insists that one can be any gender you desire in the name of equality. It also does not allow for private ownership or profit, everything belongs to the "State" which is presumably society as a whole but in actuality is simply controlled by a group of wealthy elites and the rest of the population is reduced to serfdom. When all property is deemed as belonging to all the population the acceptance of thievery is more readily shrugged off, Hollywood has exploited this in recent times with movies that feature clever criminals as the hero.

The atheist decided on another tack, "Religion is just a myth there is no proof and it is completely unscientific." "That is where you are wrong the science is often hidden in allegory, but the proof is also provided by the Bible. If we simply assume that from an ancient perspective the science was unintelligible to the early prophets and ancestors obviously explaining it would have been impossible, so they explained to the best of their ability in the language of the day. The proof however is far more definitive and is found in chapter 18 of Deuteronomy where it says that the Almighty will send prophets and if what a prophet says comes to pass we will know it is from the Lord but if it doesn't come to pass the prophet has spoken presumptuously.

Did you know that about seventy percent of the Bible is prophecy and that a good many of these have already come to pass? Demonstrating that at least seventy percent of the Bible is provably from God and not simply the presumptuous writings of men." There was obvious hesitation as he considered the idea before he said, "What prophecies have occurred?" "There are a number but there are also just as many attempts to explain or discredit prophecies.

Apostasy of the Earthmen

One early one which still raises questions and disputes is Ezekiel's prophecy regarding Tyre, he threatened Tyre with destruction and attacks from many nations but history records only two significant attacks after Ezekiel's time. The first was by Nebuchadnezzar and the second one by Alexander the great, Tyre was a city of two parts a city on the land and a city on an island offshore. When under attack the residents of Tyre would seek refuge on their island fortress and return when the enemy had left.

They did this when attacked by Nebuchadnezzar who destroyed the land-based city but could not touch the island city. Ezekiel's prophecy said the city would be thrown into the sea and fishermen would cast their nets over it. When Alexander the Great laid siege the inhabitants thought they would do what they had always done and seek refuge on their island, but Alexander was not to be thwarted.

He had his men dismantle every part of the land-based city and throw it into the sea building a causeway to the island which he then sacked and destroyed. Today fishermen can be seen casting their nets over the ruins of Tyre as predicted by the prophet." The atheist was obviously somewhat interested but I knew this one little incident was never going to sway him, convincing an atheist is like converting someone to a new religion he needs to change his paradigm: his whole belief system.

Apostasy of the Earthmen

"The more interesting of predictions are those regarding the Jewish people." "How so?" "The Bible predicted that the Jews would be "scattered among the nations" but would return to their ancient homeland "in the days of the end". The Romans had no intention of fulfilling Biblical prophecy in 70 CE when they destroyed the Temple at Jerusalem and drove the Jews from their ancient homeland, forbidding them to return.

Thus, started almost 2,000 years of one of the most amazing stories ever imagined. No people driven from their homeland and spread among many nations has ever returned after almost two thousand years and reclaimed their homeland.

The story of that return is astounding enough but the very nature of it and the prophecies that have been fulfilled by it are even more amazing. It was predicted that in the absence of the Jews the land would become barren and desolate and could not bloom again until the Jews returned. The prophecies also said that a witness would attest to this and a man would measure the city, both of these things happened, would you believe, at exactly the time at which the Jews would be enabled to return to their ancestral home. It all happened in a single year that these prophecies were fulfilled at once.

The year was 1867 and the Ottoman Empire was in dire financial straits, so they relaxed their strict rules about not selling to non-residents or foreigners. In the same year American travel writer Mark Twain visited the Holy

Apostasy of the Earthmen

Land and wrote of its barrenness and desolation and that in many miles of travel there was not a house to be seen only a few wandering Bedouins with their tents and camels.

Many Jews who would have liked to own a piece of their ancestral home were then able to buy it because of the Ottoman's desperation. Despite the poor reports from Mark Twain many Jews had the confidence in the prophecy to invest and Jewish organisations supported them. During the time that Mark Twain was touring the land so too was British Engineer Charles Warren who surveyed the land and discovered and recorded the ancient paths and boundaries of Jerusalem. All these people and events were prophesied in the Bible and none of the people involved had any idea that they were fulfilling prophecy, in fact some like Mark Twain were not religious and even sceptical about the Bible."

Apostasy of the Earthmen

Chapter 2

The atheist was obviously intrigued at the thought that there was proof of the veracity of the Bible and maybe proof of the existence of God, this was a concept he had never considered at all possible. His argument had been stopped while he thought about it and he obviously wanted time to think and maybe even check the truth of my arguments. He then asked if I would be prepared to meet and discuss the ideas with some of his friends, now the only thing worse than an argument with an atheist is a debate with a whole group of atheists. Being a glutton for punishment and because I was sure of my knowledge I agreed to the challenge.

It was a week later when I received the invitation to a restaurant in town and accepted. It was arranged to meet for lunch as the restaurant had a private room which we could have for the whole afternoon and large enough to observe social distancing as was required by law these days. They obviously intended a lengthy cross examination. The four guests who were there were friendly and all under thirty, much younger than I, which I assumed would be the case because in recent years Biblical history and religious studies had been ignored or downright ridiculed by academia.

The leftist press and those promoting literature concentrated on and promoted works that tried to explain the Biblical narrative as an impossibility and the musings of ancient illiterate people. Following introductions and pleasantries menus were passed out then drinks were ordered two guests decided to just have a beer the others agreed to share a bottle of wine with me.

Sitting back with our first drinks it did not take long for some discussion to start and naturally my declaration that Biblical prophecy was proof of the Bible's veracity had been discussed. I expected that might be the opening of discussion but instead it began with an outright challenge, "If you believe in the Bible do you really believe that the world was created only six thousand years ago?"

"I believe that the world may well have been remade only six thousand years ago. There is evidence that humans like us have lived on Earth for up to two hundred thousand years, but our history only records the last six thousand years. In that time, we have gone from caves and minimal agriculture to landing a man on the moon. I know some claim that the moon landing never happened but there are also those who claim the Earth is flat, a claim so ridiculous it can be easily disproved. A person who lives in the high country where I grew up can see that every day, whichever mountain you climb always appears to be the highest, that can only happen if the Earth is curved or only the highest would always appear highest.

Travelling to a different hemisphere will also demonstrate that the Earth is sphere. In the Northern Hemisphere the Moon's North Pole appears to be the top but, in the South the Moon's South Pole appears to be top. The Pole Star can only be seen from the North and the Southern Cross can only be seen in the South. I find it hard to believe that if man has been here for two hundred thousand years we spent one hundred and ninety-four thousands of those years without making any progress and had to wait until the last six thousand years to decide to make any advancement."

"Doesn't the Bible say that the Earth was made in only six days?" "Yes, but we know that in a way that was figurative, because according to the story the sun and moon were not made until the fourth day, so how did they measure the first days? An interesting point of that is that in the Biblical creation the sun and moon only existed in the last third of the creation. Scientists ascertain that the universe is about fifteen billion years old and the sun is only about five billion, so the sun has only existed in the last third of the life of the universe, just as recorded in the Bible.

Another story that I find interesting goes back to ancient legends that claim the Creator remakes the world every seven thousand years, but after six thousand years there is a millennium of rest, a thousand-year Sabbath of peace. This must be a worry for us because we are almost at the six-thousand-year mark. One of the Greek historians, I forget which one, wrote that when he was studying at the great library at Alexandria an Egyptian scholar said to him, "You Greeks think you are an ancient people but you have not even lived through one remake of the world, but Egypt has existed for two"."

The antagonism of the group seemed to have waned, whether it was the drinks, or I had sparked genuine interest only time would tell. The next question was more out of curiosity than as an accusation as the previous question had been, "Scientists don't believe in the Bible, do they?" "You might be surprised a great number of physicists do believe the universe shows evidence of intelligent design it is so well balanced between energy and forces it is impossible to think it could happen by accident. Who is the greatest scientist you know of?"

The response was unanimous, "Albert Einstein" although a couple of guests had replied promptly the others simply concurred. "Do you know what Einstein had to say about religion?" Shrugs and head shakes were the answers this time and so I said, "According to Einstein, Everything is determined, the beginning as well as the end, by forces over which we have no control. It is determined for the insect, as well as for the star. Human beings, vegetables, or cosmic dust, we all dance to a mysterious tune, intoned in the distance by an invisible piper."

He also said, "We are in the position of a little child, entering a huge library whose walls are covered to the ceiling with books in many different tongues. The child knows that someone must have written those books. It does not know who or how. It does not understand the languages in which they are written. The child notes a definite plan in the arrangement of the books, a mysterious order, which it does not comprehend, but only dimly suspects. That, it seems to me, is the attitude of the human mind, even the greatest and most cultured, toward God.

We see a universe marvellously arranged, obeying certain laws, but we understand the laws only dimly. Our limited minds cannot grasp the mysterious force that sways the constellations." And "Everyone who is seriously involved in the pursuit of science becomes convinced that a spirit is manifest in the laws of the Universe-a spirit vastly superior to that of man, and one in the face of which we with our modest powers must feel humble."

I was grateful that I had remembered those quotes because it seemed to be well received, if a great renowned scientist such as Einstein gave credence to a spiritual realm who were they to argue. It appeared that at least now we had some interest and minds opening to the possibility that their teachers had omitted some very pertinent facts. It still did not stop one guest from stating, "Einstein was a Jew like you, is it just that Jews are religious and learn all this from an early age?"

I replied, "You don't have to be religious to be a Jew; many Jews are secular and have little or no interest in religion." "Then how come they are Jews?" "The Bible describes Jews as B'nai Israel or the children of Israel. Meaning they are all descended from Jacob whom God renamed Israel." "But they are the 'chosen people'." "They were only chosen to receive the Torah, or God's law and to serve God, after being redeemed from slavery in Egypt, but even then, they had to accept God first.

By placing the blood of the lamb on the door post they chose to show that they were willing to obey God's commands. God did not need the blood on the door he knows where you live but there had to be declaration of obedience to God's laws, and that was the real purpose of putting the blood on the door. Not all the slaves did put the blood on the door some preferred to remain in Egypt where although they were slaves, they had food and shelter and they did not have to face the rigours of the desert. They may not have believed that Moses brought God's word or that it would be worth the effort.

To some the option may not have seemed like a bargain for God's message to Pharaoh was, "Let my people go, that they may serve me." It became a choice stay in Egypt and serve Pharaoh or go into the desert and serve God. Four hundred years of slavery had conditioned many to simply accept their life as normal. We all have choices like this every day, but we have to seek the truth because it is often hidden, what is easy may not be right."

"If the Jews are God's people how come they became slaves in Egypt?" "Karma; it began with Joseph of the coat of many colours and his dreams of seeing himself as a prince over his brothers. They felt he was such a little upstart they were going to kill him but when the opportunity came to sell him instead, he was sold as a slave. If you commit a crime like that you must pay for it and so consequently the whole tribe was led into slavery."

Chapter 3

The next question was the one with which I had expected the conversation to begin. "Do you really believe in this prophecy stuff, that someone can know the future before it happens?" I responded, "The Bible assures us that God exists unbounded by time he can therefore enable people to see that which is yet to happen, we have also heard from time to time of someone who dreamed the lottery numbers or a winning horse. Some psychologists believe everyone has precognitive dreams from time to time there are many books and papers on the phenomenon.

Experiments were conducted in which people were wired up to check their brain waves, emotions, and responses to various stimuli. They were then shown a series of images some pleasant and benign others of traumatic scenes the reactions were almost universal, and people responded negatively to the traumatic images moments before the image was displayed.

There are also experiments running what scientists call Random Event Generators there are several running in different places in the world and they appear to predict the future. The generator randomly flips either positive or negative and the norm is to produce fifty percent each way but just before a major catastrophe the generators skew one way or the other and produce either a whole string of positives or a string of negatives. The result was seen prior to the death of Princess Diana, before 9/11 and before a tsunami that killed over two hundred and fifty thousand people.

There are also records of non-Biblical prophets who have made many accurate predictions, a lot of people do not want to acknowledge this because it threatens their materialistic view of the world and the thought of having to one day account for their deeds terrifies many, as well it should. If prophecy is real it means that the view of a material universe as a giant machine spinning through space with no guidance and man as a pinnacle of evolution on this planet has no need to do other than as his heart desires, with no consequences save what society and his fellow man impose upon him. To think that there are rules that transcend a person's desires is a very worrying idea for some people.

The best known of these non-Biblical prophets is probably Nostradamus and there have been countless books written about his predictions. There are several predictions from Nostradamus that I find quite conclusive, he did mention Pasteur by name, and he named the prosecutor in the Dreyfus case a famous French trial. Many of his predictions have been open to interpretation and this has led to questions being asked, but I feel that some that are yet to be fulfilled have been interpreted to fit other events.

A prophet that I also find fascinating is the fifteenth century woman known as Mother Shipton, who was eventually burned at the stake as a witch, an event she

Apostasy of the Earthmen

predicted. Mother Shipton was impressive because she not only predicted world events but accurately described women's fashion, of which she disproved, and everything from global communication, air travel, submarines, and even mechanical farming. She also predicted a war with China and a fascinating prediction about a biological agent used in the attempt to overpower the world." At this time, I took out my smart phone and searched Mother Shipton to quote the exact verse from her writings. They were all intrigued to read,

And yellow men great power gain
From mighty bear with whom they've lain.
These mighty tyrants will fail to do
They fail to split the world in two.

But from their acts, a danger bred
An ague - leaving many dead.
And physics find no remedy
For this is worse than leprosy.

"This prophecy seems to somewhat fit Covid-19 but the worse than leprosy claim is worrying as there may be more information or something worse to come and Mother Shipton blames China and the Russian bear. She also predicts a "dragon" in the sky that threatens for seven days, which is interesting because Nostradamus also has a prediction of a star that blazes for seven days and is equal to the sun in size and brightness or in his exact words "the sun appears double".

Apostasy of the Earthmen

Another non-Biblical prophet of note is the Catholic priest St Malachy who had a vision of all the popes from his time until Judgement Day, he was born in 1094 and lived until 1148 so the list is extensive and appears quite accurate. The concerning thing for us today is that he nominated the current pope as the final pope on his list. Should St. Malachy be correct we are staring at the end of days during the lifetime of the current pope."

The waiter arrived with our meals and the conversation subsided while we ate with only a few comments between the guests who seemed to have discovered a whole new subject to consider and discuss. More drinks were ordered, and I realised that despite my long-winded explanation we had had little to drink. It was a good sign and an indication that I had held their interest with my explanation.

After we had finished eating the waiter appeared promptly to enquire about dessert orders and everybody agreed that a fruit and cheese platter would be sufficient. I had wisely chosen the fish for lunch and did not have to worry about mixing meat and dairy although some of the guests were quite comfortable and not observing a Kosher diet. I realised from this that they were probably mostly from a Christian upbringing whether they were observant in their faith or secular. The conversations continued a little longer as they all enjoyed a little more to drink and I was quite happy to allow a little discussion but knew that soon there would be another question,

Apostasy of the Earthmen

The question came and it was framed in an aggressive tone, "Do you really think that because a few predictions have come true it is evidence and not just coincidence?" "I know it is hard for you to believe even if scientists are saying something has happened and I can't really convince you, but I know because I have personal experience.

Apostasy of the Earthmen

Chapter 4

The statement brought a sudden stop to all comments and activity and all eyes turned questioningly toward me, I felt obliged to elaborate. "Yes, I am one of those people who experience both precognitory and premonitory dreams and visions, not all the time or even that often but sometimes they are very distinct and different from ordinary dreams. The thing that annoys me is that when I see the Lotto numbers, I can only ever remember four or five of them when I wake up and not enough for the major prize."

Then a guest asked, "What is it like to see the future and how long have you been able to do this?" "It is something I have had as long as I can remember, it never seemed strange and I never discussed it with anyone until I had a dream of a new little brother, my Mother with a new green washing machine, yes once upon a time washing machines were enamel and came in several colours. In the dream my little brother was towing along a little wooden horse on wheels.

I promptly forgot the dream because it was not that interesting. About two years later when I did have a little brother, I also had a part-time job looking after the hens for a local egg producer. I was paid £5 per week, a particularly good wage for a boy as the adult wage for a man was only £10 per week. It meant that when the holidays came, I was able to buy gifts for the whole family and among the gifts I chose one for my little brother it was a little wooden horse on wheels.

I had long since forgotten my dream of over two years ago and never gave it a thought. Some months later I came home from school and when I went to let my Mother know I was home I walked into the laundry and there right in front of me was the exact scene I had dreamed over two years before, I stopped in my tracks quite surprised at the accuracy and detail of what I had dreamed.

My Mother must have noticed the astonished look on my face because she asked what the matter was, I tried to explain that I was seeing a scene I had dreamed before the baby was born right down to the little wooden horse. Her only explanation was that I only bought the horse because of the dream. Maybe subconsciously I had chosen that toy because of the dream but I had nothing to do with the baby or the washing machine but it was obviously something she was not comfortable discussing so I did not push the matter.

While I was still young, I discovered I could allow my mind to relax and reach out to know what the neighbours were talking about or other people around. It was as though I was floating above them, and they were tiny little people. I gleaned a lot of things that often I did not even fully understand and one day my Father and Mother were discussing a business problem they had and although I did not understand it, I knew the answer. I mentioned it to my Father and told him what he needed to do and although I expected thanks for having the answer he just looked at me astounded and said, "Who told you that?"

At about eight or nine years of age I had no clue why that would concern him and no idea how to explain it to him, the best I could offer was, "The voices, you know like little people who live under the bed." He had a horrified look that I could not understand so I just wandered off to my room to read. Later that night my parents were discussing my advice and my Father said I was right but he didn't know how I knew and was concerned that I heard "voices" and that maybe I should see a doctor. My Mother agreed that I knew more than I should have but she suggested that they should just keep an eye on me for a while, it was at this moment I realised that not everyone could see or hear these things. From that time on I became very wary about what I could tell people."

One of the guests who had been sitting very quietly then asked a question, almost shyly, "What's it like when you have a vision or a dream?" Thinking for only a moment I replied, "Sometimes you don't even quite realise it is something from the future, I will give you an example. My wife and I have operated several businesses and at one time leased a building with reception and office in the front and a dwelling at the rear then one day I was asked 'what was this before you had it?' I thought for a moment and 'remembered' a sign out the front that said 'surveyor' and I said I thought that was what it had been.

Sometime later we had the maintenance man in to do some work and I asked him if it had been a surveyor's office before, we moved in but he said no it has only ever been an insurance office. I was a little surprised by his answer but just assumed I had been wrong and seen the sign somewhere else. A year later we took over management of a hotel and left that building. Later when I drove past there in front was the surveyor's sign, I believed I had remembered years earlier. My memory was of the future and not the past" I then embarrassed the guest by asking what he had foreseen, he flushed but did not say anything so I quickly said, "That's OK it doesn't matter." We were both aware that he had experienced something psychic, but I am not sure if anyone else picked up on the exchange.

"I am sure of many of these things because I too have had dreams and visions of some of the predictions recorded by the prophets. Star or dragon, maybe a comet predicted by both Nostradamus and Mother Shipton I have seen in a dream, but I believed it might have been a supernova shining as bright as the sun. In my dream I was standing by my front gate watching it rise in the East and a neighbour approached and asked if I thought this was the end of the world, but I told him not for a little while yet, which he accepted." Then the fruit and cheese platter arrived, and the waiter took orders for coffee.

Apostasy of the Earthmen

Apostasy of the Earthmen

Chapter 5

We all chose fruit or cheese to our liking and then my atheist friend who had arranged the lunch said, "I think you have given some good examples of precognition but does that really prove the existence of God?" I responded, "According to the Bible prophecy does come from God and we cannot deny that so many of the Biblical prophecies have been fulfilled and in the allotted time according to the laws of the Jubilees set down in Biblical law".

He then responded, "But I have a problem believing that there is some sort of fairy in the sky or some be-whiskered old gentleman as painted by Michelangelo." I said, "That's the problem there. Those images are the legacy of a pagan past and come from the Greco-Roman history of "Gods" that are just people. It started with the Greek God Kronos who was concerned about a prophecy that said his son would kill him and take his crown.

To ensure this did not happen he ate his children until the Mother hid a son from him, that son did grow up to kill his Father and take the throne. He cut his father open and rescued his siblings who were still alive in the father's stomach. That son was called Zeus by the Greeks and Jupiter by the Romans and has nothing to do with the Creator God of the Bible. The God of the Bible has no corporeal existence he is the Lord of the Spirits imagine if you will that the universe itself is cognisant. It has an intelligent awareness of its own existence.

Apostasy of the Earthmen

That is what the God of the Bible is like, an aware universe whose consciousness creates and controls all matter and existence, even the flow of time. The moment of creation began with that awareness, the realisation of existence the "I am" moment. The "Let there be light" moment began the first fusion of hydrogen atoms into something else and the energy released became the heat and light of the first stars. The evolution of the universe grew from that and during that whole time the universe was aware and growing into what it could become.

The Bible tells us that God is outside time so is not affected by how the universe evolves but whether all the knowledge existed at the moment of creation or whether it has grown since, I have no clue. If it has been increasing since the beginning that can be an awful lot of knowledge accrued in fifteen billion years. It may be that the universe is older than that because there are stars that appear to be older than the universe. This of course is one of the things that has scientists questioning the big bang theory. The Methuselah star only two hundred light years from Earth seems to be about twenty million years older than the entire universe. It may well be that all our beliefs about the structure of the universe are wrong, or incomplete."

Scientists have discovered anomalies in the fine alpha structure of the universe and even in the speed of light or the rate of causality. It seems that many of the things of which we were once certain may in fact be erroneous. There is even conjecture that the universe might be holographic in nature, being somehow generated and sustained by some force from outside the physical boundaries of the universe. Strangely this reflects the Biblical description of a universe created and sustained by an unseen creator.

The more we discover about cosmology and physics the more it indicates that the description from the Bible may have a basis in fact, but as for your question about whether we can produce an "essence of God" in a test tube or some easily verifiable experiment it does not appear to be possible and most cannot or won't try to understand the level of mathematics that inspires many scientists to suspect that there is something complicated and unseen happening in the universe."

At this point another of the guests interjected and asked, "Do you believe in God because of the mathematics or because of faith or your religion?" "Not entirely," I replied, "I explained that I have precognitive dreams and visions these indicate to me that something is going on, but I was once very blasé about religion and paid little attention. I had read the scriptures in my youth and had a glimpse that this was going to come about in my lifetime but apart from that I filed it away and promptly went on with my life.

As a young man I was active in many sports and quite good at several, but I also enjoyed cars and motorcycles, women, and wine. I tried to fit in more living than I really had time for but still studied hard because I was interested in science, particularly physics regarding the nature of time. I knew that if I could see the future, our understanding of time was incomplete at best or downright wrong at worst. I also became interested in the new theory of electronic data processing or I.T. as we call it today.

I studied business management and accounting and began to develop ways to do these things by computer and soon found myself designing systems for corporate computing. This became my life for the next twenty years, I was mixing in the corporate world of high flyers I had a wife and family and what time wasn't at work or study was often with the family, my interest in religion and the nature of time took a back seat to my ever increasing family and business interests.

Eventually my health started to catch up with me and when the company I was working for was taken over I took a retirement package and bought my first business. It was sometime after running this business for a couple of years we took a holiday but during this time I caught a chest infection, my asthma became serious and I rushed to the local medical centre. It was there that I suffered a respiratory arrest and experienced an out of body event. My wife saw me collapse and pulled me upright to get air into my lungs and at that moment the nurse arrived with oxygen mask and medication, I found myself sinking back into my body and immediately became aware of my physical weight.

Apostasy of the Earthmen

This was an experience that had me thinking again about the nature of reality and our place in it. An even more interesting near-death experience was waiting for me again a couple of years later. This time I was completely gone I was in the light and up above talking to God, I was aware of my body back in the bed but was fascinated by where I was and I had heard people who had similar experiences say "you can feel the love" in my experience you can feel everything.

It was a feeling of total empathy you can feel the emotion of the Almighty, I would hate to arrive up there if he were displeased with me, I think that would be total agony. I naturally had to ask, "Why did you create us?" I am not the only one apparently to ask about the meaning of life and the emotion I received back was not merely a feeling of love but of a good humour as if I was a child asking why water is wet or something similar.

The answer came back that inanimate objects can be made with a whim, but how else can a spirit make beings like him? I realised he looks on us as his children and our spirit or soul is his offspring. I realised what a lonely place the universe must be if you were the only living soul in it. I did not have time to discuss all I would like to know because I was being sent back and was being revived. The adrenaline injection kicked in and a warm feeling flooded my body and I started to breathe and so did the medical staff.

Apostasy of the Earthmen

Hydro-cortisone intravenous shot and some other medication and I was breathing evenly and went to sleep, I awoke some hours later and my wife some family and friends were standing around me and I realised that I was in the palliative care unit. I said, "They've put me in with the sick old people." One visitor simply replied, "Look in the mirror." It was after that I started to pay attention to religion and began to be observant, to read the scriptures and to begin to pray as we are supposed to do.

Chapter 6

My stories had aroused the interest of my audience, but I had no idea what they thought of my explanations. The next question showed that they were giving things some thought, "Jews don't believe in Jesus, do they?" "That's not quite correct Jews have ample evidence of Jesus. He lived two thousand years ago, and his followers have been responsible for countless pogroms, Crusades, Inquisitions, and the Holocaust that is how Jews have been taught about Jesus.

It is a shame really because Jesus was a Jew and taught the Torah, in fact one of the earliest statements attributed to Jesus is that he said in Matthew 5:17-18 "Think not that I am come to destroy the law, or the prophets. I am not come to destroy but to fulfil. For verily I say to you till Heaven and Earth pass not one jot or tittle shall in no wise pass from the law until all be fulfilled." That is using the common translation in the King James Bible, he probably actually said not one yud, which is the smallest letter in the Hebrew aleph bet and looks a bit like an apostrophe. Jesus' followers modified the law, particularly the Romans who aligned the Jewish rituals with their worship of Jupiter and the pagan gods they followed."

"You make Christianity sound particularly evil." "It is not Christianity that is evil it is the men who have distorted the teachings of Jesus to achieve their own ends. Therefore, many people make comments like the one that led us to this lunch, that religion is the the cause of all the world's problems. It is not religion that is wrong or even the teachings of the Bible or Jesus but all that has come from men who are zealots and pushing their own often mistaken view of the Bible and salvation."

"But Jesus is the Messiah!" Came the complaint, to which I responded, "Why do you believe that?" "Because it's in the Bible?" "Well! Let us examine what the Bible says about the Messiah, the Messiah is predicted by the prophets Isaiah, Jeremiah and Ezekiel and there are five things that are predicted to happen when the Messiah arrives. First is universal peace as Isaiah says, "He shall rebuke many people and they shall beat their swords into ploughshares and their spears into pruning hooks: nation shall not rise up against nation neither shall they learn war anymore."

Since the time of Jesus, the world has experienced nine years of war for every one year of peace so that prediction certainly has not been fulfilled. Secondly the spirit of the Lord will be poured out on all men and there shall be a universal knowledge of God, if that had happened, we would not be at this lunch. The third prophecy is that all the Jews will be gathered into the Holy Land to serve God, where he will make them prosper. Today about half the world's Jews are in Israel and more are returning everyday so that is still not fulfilled.

Apostasy of the Earthmen

The fourth prophecy to be fulfilled at the coming of the Messiah is the rebuilding of the Temple at Jerusalem, at present Jews are not even permitted to pray on the Temple Mount because it is occupied by Muslims who forbid Jewish prayer. The fifth prophecy to occur is the restoration of a descendent of King David to the throne of Israel that is still not fulfilled."

One guest who had sat quietly making no comment and asking no questions then found the courage to join the conversation. "Then if Jesus hasn't fulfilled the requirements to be the Messiah how come they call him the saviour?" "That's a very interesting question and one that I and many others have considered, Jesus is also sometimes referred to as "the lamb of God". We know that in the past a lamb was offered as a sacrifice for the remission of sin, it may be that Jesus was chosen to be a sacrifice for the remission of the world's sins.

Despite the view of many that Jesus is God we should remember that according to prophecy the Messiah is a man. Jesus also denied that he was God in Matthew 19:17 when he said, "... why thou callest me good there is none good but one that is God." The name Jesus in Hebrew is Yeshua which means salvation and Isaiah chapter 53 does seem to indicate a saviour who many assume is Jesus he is described as, "A man of sorrows" sent to accept the punishment for sin. It is also claimed that Jesus rose from the grave and ascended to Heaven to sit at the right hand of God, which indicates he is not God but a separate being, unless we assume that God is beside himself, which given the mess we have made of his creation might be understandable.

The willingness to sacrifice a son goes back to Abraham who was willing to sacrifice his son to please God, it may be that God is prepared to return the favour to save us. The crucifixion of Jesus has parallels in the ancient Yom Kippur ritual where two kids are brought to be sacrificed on the day of Atonement and one is chosen by lot while the other is taken outside the city and released. In Jesus case there were two, Jesus and Barabbas, one was released and the other, an innocent man, was sacrificed for the remission of sin.

Regardless of whether Jesus was or was not God's choice as a sacrifice or considered to be the Messiah he has not fulfilled the prophecies, but he may well represent an atonement for our sins. There is a question raised by Ezekiel 43, that says that the Messiah will bring a bull as a sacrifice in the Temple. This implies two things, first that the Temple will be rebuilt and second that the Messiah will still need to offer a sacrifice, which means that Jesus death has not absolved humanity for all time.

As a Jew I still have the view that scripture assures us that God is the Creator and sustainer of the universe the Messiah is just a man. God has no corporeal body he is a spirit a force and there is none like him. We are guided by the first Commandment wherein we were ordered to obey, "I am the Lord your God who redeemed you from slavery in Egypt, you shall have no other God but me." A definite statement of law by which we are all bound.

This is just my opinion, but I think many have assumed that Jesus will save them just by dying, but he did warn that you would be judged by the way you treat your fellow man. You cannot be a murderer and a thief and expect to escape judgement just because Jesus died. As in Judaism Christians must endeavour to right wrongs and repent of misdeeds and to make atonement through good works and charity. It is also necessary to acknowledge God and to pray for forgiveness, you will not receive it if you don't ask for it."

In Hebrew we pray to Avinu Malkeinu, our Father our King for forgiveness and mercy. Not in the merit of our righteousness do we seek redemption but from his abundant mercy. In Christianity Jesus taught people to pray to "Our Father In Heaven" at no time did he instruct people to pray to, "Me and my Mum and Dad". His instructions are a two-edged sword, "Forgive us our trespasses as we forgive those who trespass against us." In this statement you are asking to be forgiven in the same measure as you forgive others, which seems fair, if you cannot be forgiving you should not expect forgiveness.

I paused for a moment, wondering if they were all falling asleep after my long-winded talk, but as they appeared to be still interested. I asked, "Do you guys want to take a break and then talk some more or call it quits for now?"

Apostasy of the Earthmen

There was a little low chatter and then the fellow who had put the group together said, "We should take a break and see if most of us want to hear more or come back another day."

During the break we ordered more coffee, and everyone took the opportunity to stretch their legs and walk around a little, informally chatting to each other. If they wished to extend today's discussion at least they would be alert when I resumed. It was not to be however, for the group decided that they would like to leave further discussion for a future date, I was surprised when they asked if I would be free to join them for lunch the following week.

I agreed if the venue was available and so the enquiries were made, and a booking confirmed. It was a pleasant enough venue and the group had turned out to be quite open minded and eventually not at all aggressive or antagonistic, showing quite an interest in learning and in finding the truth. I secretly chastised myself for thinking the worst of these young men and expecting confrontation. I resolved to thank them in the future for their openness and courtesy, it is too easy to judge others when you don't know them and I had assumed that because they were basically atheists they would be adverse to anything that might question their paradigm.

We often assume the young are totally indoctrinated by the "God is dead" attitude of academics. When many have had doubts about the veracity of their teachers claims and are not eager to embrace the immorality of those who oppose religion in all its forms. Many have a conscience and feel uncomfortable when faced with sexual deviance and other attitudes of promiscuity and dishonesty they are willing to learn what is right and good.

Apostasy of the Earthmen

Chapter 7

The following week I arrived for the lunch I was surprised to find a larger group, some had brought girl friends or partners, looking around I noticed the faces from the previous week and asked jokingly, "Am I in the right place?" The instigator of the original lunch spoke up, "We have been talking about the stuff you said last week, some of us have even started to read the Bible to find out what it is all about. We have been talking about it all and now some friends and partners have become interested, you made more sense just talking than all the church services we have ever seen."

"The difference is that I am not following a ritual and preaching a sermon, simply talking about what I know in relation to scripture and the world today." The group mingled most of them knew each other but there were a few introductions and I was the only stranger without any previous connection with any other guest, except those who had been at lunch the previous week.

Drinks were ordered and guests arranged themselves around the table, some side discussions were going on and menus were passed out by the waiter. There was a little silence while choices were made, I took the time to look at the group and noticed that the little dining room was almost at capacity. It was obvious that if these discussions were going to continue and numbers increase, we would be looking for a new venue as this one had almost reached the permissible limit. I did not think I had too much more to teach them we should end soon unless we moved onto another topic.

I had wondered how this might start, whether guests had questions or were waiting for me to raise a topic, but the meals arrived, and everybody ate lunch after which one of the guests from the previous week began. "Last week you mentioned how Jews have learned of Jesus from the persecution by Christians, what about Muslims?"

"Interesting that you should ask that, some time ago a friend said to me Judaism has been the root of two new religions and both are trying to kill us. It is not all Christians and not all Muslims that want to kill Jews but enough to make life difficult. I have good friends who are Muslim and who are educated enough to know the history. That Islam and Judaism both began with Abraham and his sons. Ishmael was the eldest and Isaac the younger, but it was through Isaac that God said he would pass down Abraham's legacy.

The reason that the younger was special is because although God had promised Abraham that he would be the father of many nations and because they were old they did not have the faith in God to wait, so his wife Sarah gave Abraham her handmaiden to beget a son, thus Ishmael was born. Some years later the Lord visited and told Sarah who was already ninety years old that next year she would have a son and as predicted Isaac was born the next year.

Apostasy of the Earthmen

Therefore, Isaac was granted precedence over Ishmael, because he was born due to an act of God. Following the death of Sarah Abraham married Keturah and had a further six sons but without God's assistance. When Abraham eventually died Ishmael, Isaac, and the sons of Keturah buried him in the cave he had bought as a tomb for Sarah. The tomb of the patriarchs is a sacred site in Israel venerated by both Muslims and Jews. The brothers were friends and agreed on the allocation of the lands, it is only since the days of Muhammad that Muslims have tried to conquer all the lands.

Prior to Muhammad producing the Koran the Laws of Noah were the sole guide for all of Abraham's descendants. The full name of the Torah is Sefer Ha Torah, which means the Book of the Law. The Torah according to tradition was dictated to Moses by God prior to this the descendants of Abraham observed what were called the Noahide Laws which were the laws Noah received and passed on after the flood. There were only seven commandments, but they did include worship only God, do not murder, do not steal, do not lie, which are the very basics for a civil society.

The Gospel or the story of Jesus was never meant to change the Torah, but the Koran was designed to replace them both. So, without the various translations and interpretations all people should be worshipping and praying to the God of the Bible. The prophets and teachers should be remembered, and their teachings observed but they are not Gods to be worshipped. A prophet or leader should only teach what is in the Bible to add or teach that it is false is blasphemy. It is one thing to go astray yourself but to lead others astray is an abomination."

One of the new guests asked, "Do you think we will all be judged on whether we are good or evil?" "It is prophesied, and I have no doubt, but it might not be as many people imagine. Having been dead and experienced the beyond I think just the experience of being aware of your shortcomings would be a terrible burden and painful. You missed my explanation last week but being in the presence of the Almighty can be an uplifting feeling but if you were to incur his displeasure it would be mortifying but if you are already dead there is no escape." She responded, "I was told the story of your experience, and that is why I came today."

"Is that the only thing you found interesting?" "It was something tangible and a firsthand experience along with your precognition." "Are you looking for answers or for guidance, in other words are you worried about living or dying?" "I was worried about the future will we live, or will we die?" "Everybody dies eventually we just hope it won't be for a while yet and that during our life we manage to do the right thing, and then we need have no fear of death. We just hope that it is peaceful and painless, nobody wants to go in a fiery blast or devastating accident."

Apostasy of the Earthmen

"I also wondered about reincarnation; do you think that is possible?" "I think it is very probable, there are a couple of Biblical verses that indicate that it does happen. The prophet Malachi says in one of his last statements that God said, "Behold I will send you Elijah the prophet before the coming of the great and dreadful day of the Lord. (Malachi 4:5). There is also a prophecy about the prophet Elias, this is just the Greek form of the name Elijah, coming before the Messiah and when the disciples asked Jesus about this he said Elias is come already and they recognised him not. The disciples understood that he referred to John the Baptist, (Matthew 17:10-13). Jesus apparently believed that John the Baptist was Elijah reincarnated. If we are all reincarnated souls it makes the resurrection of the dead something different to what most expect. Instead of people popping up out of the ground we could have sudden recall of our previous lives and the dead would be living again."

That concept caused a period of silence as they thought about the possibilities, and then came another question, "What do you personally think of reincarnation?" "Well I think it is more likely than not, there have been many reports of children accurately remembering past lives, an ability we seem to lose at about age five. In my younger days I used to have a repetitive dream in which I was being chased by soldiers, in my dream I was about twenty years of age and was out running them easily.

They had fired shots toward me, but these fell short or ricocheted harmlessly past, I was only about fifty to seventy metres from the riverbank and knew that if I managed to get across the river, I would be safe. The river was obviously a border, I felt that I was going to make it but then from a different angle and much closer, came men on horseback and just as I reached the top of the bank one fired and hit me in the back sending me tumbling down the bank into the river. Next thing I knew I was looking down from above at my body lying face down in the water and thinking, "Get up you are going to drown."

The horsemen arrived at the top of the riverbank and looked down at the body face down in the water and laughed. I then realised if I was looking down from above, I was already dead and would not be able to lift my head at that realisation the dream ended. When I was young, I wondered if I might have been a native American chased and killed by cowboys but as I have grown older I realised from the uniforms of the soldiers the place probably was Europe and it could have happened during a pogrom or the Holocaust."

Then the conversation changed direction. "For a Jew you know a lot about Jesus." "Well I know that although he did not fulfill the prophecies about the Messiah, he appears to have been a sacrifice for the sins of the world. There is nothing that happens in the world that is not God's will and I did have a strange experience to do with Jesus." "What was that?" I hesitated before replying, "It is not something I discuss because it worries me that people would think it crazy and I am not even sure if or how it happened it was too unbelievable."

Apostasy of the Earthmen

Chapter 8

One of the original guests asked, "Can you tell us about it, we won't think it unbelievable." I replied, "Well we started this because some of you thought religion was the cause of all the world's problems and was just a bunch of old myths, why are you now interested in a story that to me at least seems more incredulous than anything in the Bible." "Since listening to you we have had a chance to see that some things might be possible that we had never suspected."

"Then I suppose if I was ever going to tell anyone outside my immediate family I might as well make it this group. It happened quite a few years ago, although most Jews are not hunters and have strict rules about slaughter; harts, gazelles and roebucks were hunted for King Solomon's table. I too enjoy venison, but I also hunt to destroy vermin such as feral goats, foxes, rabbits, and cats which harm our ecology and have been responsible for the destruction of numerous native species. Rabbits are dog food, but I do know people who like to eat them and when I was quite young used to sell for two bob a pair. I guess you are all too young to understand that, but two shillings was equal to twenty cents, a good price in the days a man's wage was ten pounds or twenty dollars a week.

To get back to the story I had gone out early before dawn in the days before I had become observant and prayed every morning and evening. I spent several pleasant

Apostasy of the Earthmen

hours hiking through the bush and had quite a successful hunt returning to my campsite mid-morning. I relit my fire to boil a billy to make a coffee planning coffee and biscuits before heading off on the drive home. I cleaned the game and put meat in the car fridge to take home threw some pieces in the fire and took the rest a short distance into the scrub to leave for scavengers. I then walked down to the bank of the creek to bathe and wash off the blood that had come from my butchering.

Once I was cleaned up, I made a coffee and took my cup and sat on a ledge by the creek where I had some minutes ago washed away the blood. I sat on a rock with my boots and socks beside me and finished my biscuits and coffee watching the water rippling over some small rapids and looking back at the long pool to the upstream side. It was then I heard a sound and turned to look back toward my campsite. There walking toward me was a man I did a quick double take because like me he was barefooted but was wearing a long-knitted robe like a kaftan."

"Do you know who I am?" He asked, I thought to myself, Jesus, but just said, "I think so." He said, "Come with me I want to show you something." He took me by the arm, and we took two steps to the creek and then we were standing on top of the water, it was the most stunning experience you could imagine. I could feel the water under my feet, but my feet were not getting wet, it was not soft like walking on a waterbed or hard like the ground or ice. It was cold and it was moving as we walked to the centre of the stream and I could see a school of tiny fishes swimming under my feet.

The man had been talking to me, but I was somewhat unaware of what he was saying because I was so blown away by the experience and the sensation. I eventually managed to give him some of my attention and realised he was saying, "Even Peter who saw many miracles was unable to do this but you have great faith, but you will need it." Oh great, I thought as we stepped onto the bank and I turned back to look at the creek, still having trouble believing what had just happened. I turned back to ask him to elaborate on why I would need great faith, but he was gone.

Still struggling to believe the experience I thought I had to try this again but this time my foot went straight to the bottom of the stream obviously it was not something I could do on my own. I dried off my wet foot and put my boots back on cleaned my rifle and packed my things into the car for the trip home. After extinguishing the fire I walked around the area to see if there was any evidence of my visitor but finding none I had to assume it was some sort of dream or hallucination, but the one thing that was truly unique and impossible to forget was the sensation of walking on the water and the rippling of the stream under my feet.

In reflection I could not understand why a not particularly religious Jew would have such an experience or dream growing up in a Christian country, which

Apostasy of the Earthmen

Australia was at that time, I had been exposed to the story of Jesus and movies such as "King of Kings", despite being Jewish by birth through having a Yiddish Great-grandmother we were not greatly observant of Jewish or Christian traditions. We always had two "Christmases" one at my Grandmother's house was always before the regularly observed date. It was no big deal and we never referred to it as Hanukkah, my Mother was always quiet about family ethnicity I assume that was because she was a young girl during the war and still had relatives in Germany before the war but none afterward.

Great-grandma's family were originally from Heilbronn in Germany and when Hitler came to power in 1933 it took him just three weeks to open the first concentration camp at Dachau and the first Jews, he rounded up were those from Heilbronn. We were fortunate that the family were manufacturing jewellers and had opened shops in other cities such as London, Paris, and Rome. Our great-grandparents came to Australia from London, as gold buyers during the gold rush and stayed. The sons opened other businesses that were in demand such as a flour mill and four timber mills, actions for which I am forever grateful. It would not have boded well for the family to have returned to Germany.

Although my Mother's family were Jewish, they were quite assimilated into Christian culture and although retaining many Jewish customs also adopted many of the customs of the society around them. My Paternal

Apostasy of the Earthmen

Grandfather was a member of the Plymouth Brethren which is often confused with the cult like Exclusive Brethren. As Australia was part of the British Empire the official documents of the day only recognised two religions, Church of England or "other".

My first real introduction to the difference in religions came when I was about five years of age. One of my Father's brothers married a Catholic girl who insisted the children be raised in that religion, including going to Catholic school. During the school holidays I stayed at my Uncle's for a couple of days and my cousin took me aside to tell me a secret that he had learned at school. I had no idea what could be secret about school, but I went off to a quiet spot with him where he explained his news, "the Jews killed Jesus,"

It came as bit of a shock for a five-year-old, my first thought was, "Why is he telling me, I didn't do it." My next concern was that maybe Grandpa shot him in the war because I knew he had been to France in WWI, although I now realise that as a medic my grandfather probably did not shoot anyone. You can see that by these experiences I had quite a varied introduction to different religions.

Living in a tiny rural hamlet where there were no churches religion was not a priority, although once a fortnight the Salvation Army officer from a nearby town would come out and hold a Sunday School in the school hall. He would read stories from the Bible and play the piano so we could all sing Salvation Army songs like "Onward Christian Soldiers" without really paying attention to the meaning.

All the school age children in town, except for the only Catholic family, went along because apart from Bible stories there were discussions on morality and good behaviour followed by morning tea. Biscuits and cordial in summer and hot chocolate and cake in the winter, the fire would be lit in winter and we would sit around talking. The whole meeting was more a social event for participants than a religious experience, of course the Salvation Army took up a collection which must have been worthwhile, or the service would not have continued. That is the extent of my religious education until after I had my near-death experiences and decided it was time to find out what I should know."

I stopped talking and looked around to see if there were any questions or whether my long-winded talk had lost them or sent them to sleep. I was surprised to see that they had obviously been listening and were waiting to see if I had more to add. I suggested we take a break and move around for a couple of minutes and have coffee. The guests seemed happy with this and several started their own discussions.

Apostasy of the Earthmen

Chapter 9

A guest then asked, "You said that because the Bible is two thirds prophecy, we know it is inspired by God is that the only reason we should believe?" "Well let me ask you, what do you think of the number seven?" This drew a few blank looks; it was obvious that nobody had given it any thought. "Did you know that seven is the number that signifies completion? It is mentioned hundreds of times in the Bible. We are surrounded by sevens and people never even recognise just how often or what it means.

Let me give a few examples. First and the most obvious is a seven-day week which of course was designated to acknowledge the seven days of creation with the seventh day a day of rest. The Earth has seven continents and the seas are divided by geologists into seven oceans. There are seven colours in a rainbow and seven notes in a musical scale. We can see with the naked eye seven objects in the solar system, they are the Sun, Moon, Mercury, Venus, Mars, Jupiter, and Saturn.

If these are not enough sevens there are seven levels in the periodic table of the elements and seven metals known since antiquity these are, gold, copper, silver, lead, tin, iron, and mercury. All these sevens would be simply coincidence if it were not for the Bible telling us that seven is important and relevant. Apart from the hundreds of mentions there is the symbolism of the very first verse of the Bible which implies significance.

Apostasy of the Earthmen

In English, the first verse contains ten words, but in the original Hebrew it has only seven words. The term. "in the beginning" is three words in English but in Hebrew it is Bereshit (בראשית) one word. These seven words have a total of twenty-eight letters or four times seven. The three main nouns God, Heaven and Earth contain fourteen Hebrew letters or twice seven. The smallest word appears in the middle of the sentence and the word either side of it has five letters so each of these taken with the middle word totals seven letters.

In Hebrew, the letters are numbers there is no separate index of numbers, this means that each word also has a number value, and this is known as gematria. The gematria of the three nouns God, Heaven and Earth totals seven hundred and seventy-seven or one hundred and eleven times seven. Even human life is ruled by sevens, the first seven sees the loss of milk teeth or baby teeth, the second seven brings us to puberty. The third seven brings physical maturity and by the fourth seven we reach mental maturity while the fifth brings us to mid-life at thirty-five.

The level of fitness and knowledge at mid-life determines how we age from that point on, if we have a high level of fitness and stability we can build on that to a healthy and comfortable old age, but if we are unfit and uneducated at thirty-five we will probably experience a rapid decline followed by an early death. Have a look at how many people suffer an early death at forty-two, or forty-nine, the sixth and seventh sevens. The number of

Apostasy of the Earthmen

deaths increases every year from that point, until the tenth seven or seventy years of age at which time the Bible says is our expected life span of three-score years plus ten. The Bible also says that those with strong constitutions may live to eighty years or more by good living and activity. Modern medicine has seen life expectancy in most western cultures to increase to average about eighty-one for men and eighty-three for women, so most of us can expect to surpass the Biblical age limit.

In early times Biblical scholars knew that by counting the letters in the Torah and reading only very other letter or every third or fourth or even greater jumps the names of famous kings and prophets would appear with events associated with them. Today with modern computers we are able to skip dozens or even hundreds of letters to find names and events that have been recorded in the Bible and that are happening today. This amazing system of equidistant letter skipping is commonly called the "Bible Codes" We have only discovered a small amount of the information that is in the Bible, but which proves the Bible's significance. The codes only appear in the Hebrew Bible, that is the original language.

Apostasy of the Earthmen

Chapter 10

It appeared that the guests were all still interested in hearing more ideas, and then one asked, "What about UFO's isn't there something about UFOs' in the Bible?" "Well there is conjecture that the flying machine described by Ezekiel is some sort UFO. In ancient times the knowledge of these things was limited by the lack of scientific understanding by people who were not technologically advanced they had difficulty describing what they had seen.

When Jacob earned the name Israel it was because he contended with an angel and was victorious, but he describes a "ladder" going up to Heaven on which angels were coming and going. It appears that what Jacob saw was some sort of portal, but he described it as a dream because it was not something he could explain in his waking state. We often see things as somewhat unreal when something strange or unusual happens. People who are in an accident sometimes say it was like being in a dream, or slow motion.

It does appear that in ancient times there was interaction between people on Earth and beings from somewhere else." I took a moment to look up an article I had previously read and then read the story to them. "The Louvre in Paris has a set of seven books of Kabbalist writings some of, which are quite surprising. One section describes seven inhabited worlds and provides an amazing amount of detail of these worlds particularly when we consider that the writings were prepared at a time when the population of the world thought that the Earth was flat and the centre of all creation.

The "Seven other Worlds" are as follows –

1.Geh. A world of trees. The inhabitants plant trees and their food comes from these, they have no cereal crops. This world has many large animals.

2. Nesziah. This world has a red sun, the inhabitants are exceedingly small, and their diet consists of shrubs and plants, which occur naturally, they have no agriculture. They have poor memories and have no noses but breath through two holes in their heads.

3. Thebel. This planet has different races who vary in both colour and appearance, their food comes from the water and they are superior to all other beings. The planet is a long way from the sun, and they revive their dead.

4. Erez. The inhabitants of this world are described as descendants of Adam. The name of the planet is similar to Haaretz, which is Hebrew for the Earth.

5. Adamah. The inhabitants of this world are also described as descendants of Adam; the description of this planet is the most like Earth. The inhabitants were brought here because Adam complained that Erez was dreary. The inhabitants are often unhappy, raise crops, eat meat, plants, and bread, and often make war.

Apostasy of the Earthmen

6. Arqa. The inhabitants of this world are agricultural; their faces are different from humans and they visit all worlds and speak all languages.

7. Tziah.   The inhabitants of this planet are fair of face and have more faith than all other beings. They must not eat what other beings eat. The planet has two suns and is very dry, the inhabitants continually seek underground water but there are great riches and many fine buildings on this world.

In these days of understanding the principles of space flight we can comprehend the possibility of inhabited planets, but how the authors of ancient texts could have come to this conclusion is beyond speculation. Legends also tell of a war in Heaven and ancient Gods, but we know so little. Scientists have evidence that people like us have existed on Earth for as much as two hundred thousand years but our history only goes back about five thousand years, are we to believe that for one hundred and ninety five thousand years people did nothing and then went from the caves to the moon in only five thousand years?"

Recently the United States Navy has released footage that was previously leaked showing some sort or Unidentified Flying Objects detected and filmed by fighter jets. The films were initially leaked but have since been officially released. Despite many years of hiding information, the US Navy has since admitted these things exist. The objects in the released video are too small to have been manned craft but their speed and agility is far ahead of any known Earthly technology. The US senate has since ordered the information held by the military be made available to the public. They want us to know if the Earth is being visited by aliens or inspected by alien drones.

It is only my opinion that we are being kept under observation and the reason we are not being approached is because the aliens made such a mess of contact last time they were here. If there is a force in the universe that rules Heaven and Earth it may well be forbidden to approach Earth men until such time as the Almighty deems contact appropriate. We tend to shoot first and ask questions later so in order to avoid a nuclear exchange it would be prudent for aliens to keep their distance. When the Mashiach arrives and the world is at peace under one King it might be safe for aliens to make an approach.

That observation quite obviously had them thinking and considering the amount of evidence I had been giving them, then one guest said, "You should write a book because we can never remember all this information." I responded, "I have thought about it and because it is so familiar to me I can recite most of it without effort, but I suppose a book would enable me to reach more people if you all think it interesting enough." There were was a chorus of requests and suggestions and so I said, "Seeing we have been here for a good while today would you like to keep going, or should we come back again and examine some more details of the World and the Bible.

There seemed to be a split between those who wanted to continue today and those who wanted to arrange another meeting. I suggested a break to allow them to discuss and decide, they readily agreed to this and then eventually agreed to return when they had made time to read up on the Bible and think of some more questions. I promised that in that the case, I would take the time to make notes of the things we had already discussed and prepare the outline needed to compile a book. I realised then that I should have been keeping notes or have already prepared summaries from which to deliver my talks. After checking that the venue would be available in a week the group said their goodbyes and each went off in their own direction.

Apostasy of the Earthmen

Chapter 11

The week passed and the group met again, fortunately the numbers had not grown again this week, but none had given up on the talks either. I wondered if I had inspired any to begin their own voyage of discovery, or would they simply listen for a while and go back to their secular lives. The meetings were also becoming something of a social event, and I wondered if that was the attraction or whether there was real interest in the Bible.

Once drinks were ordered and menus decided the first question demonstrated that interest was growing, when one from the original group asked, "Why is the Bible so significant?" I thought about this for a moment before replying, "I had planned to discuss prophecy and Judgement Day later because that is the culmination of all Bible teaching, but the beginning is first, the example of Noah and how God has already destroyed the world once but then worship as we know it really began with Abraham.

Because Abraham was a good man and obeyed God's will he was granted a special blessing. God said, "And I will bless them that bless thee, and curse him that curseth thee: and in thee shall all families of the earth be blessed." This is the translation given in the King James version of the bible but in the Hebrew two different words are used for the term curse. First instead of those who curse you God said וּמְקַלֶּלְךָ (ū·mə·qal·lel·ḵā) which could be translated as those who make light of you. The second word used where God says, "I will curse" is אָאֹר (a or) which could be better translated as I will eliminate/disappear or annihilate. Those who bless the descendants of Abraham will themselves be blessed but those who "make light" or treat them poorly will be no more.

In obeying God's command and being prepared to sacrifice his son a promise was made to Abraham that his descendants would be God's people and be bound to God for all time. Abraham's two oldest sons Ishmael and Isaac were the Fathers of the Arabs and the Jews, his other sons were Fathers of many people. When Abraham bound his son upon the altar God decreed that Abraham's descendants were bound to God, "Unto all generations". The only requirement is that those descendants observe God's laws. We are expected not to turn our back on the Almighty lest calamity befall the Earth; unfortunately, that is exactly what many have done, and we have become an apostate society denying the very existence of God. Don't you ever wonder why there is so much strife in the world today?"

There was a lull while meals arrived, and I took the opportunity to have something to drink and eat my meal. A guest then asked, "If the Bible and history imply that aliens have visited Earth do you think these could be angels?" I replied, "It is highly likely because although the common idea of an angel is of a Heavenly being with wings there are many variations in the Bible. There are angels and archangels, seraphim, and cherubim and not all are winged creatures in fact some have been mistaken for men. The name for angels in Hebrew means one who goes back and forth or a messenger. The angels who went to Sodom to warn Lot and his family to leave were thought of as men and the men of Sodom wanted to have sex with them, but the angels struck them all blind. It is predicted that before the day of the Lord a messenger or an angel from the East will come to bring God's word and prepare for the Messiah.

In Daniel, the one who comes first is described as "the ancient of days" implying one who is old, and Daniel describes him as having white hair and a white beard." "Like you," interjected one of the guests jokingly, "That is a worry," I replied. After the laughter subsided, I continued, "In Jewish tradition the one who comes first is the Moshiach Ben Yosef or the Messiah from the house of Joseph. The Messiah who comes to rule the world and bring about world peace is Moshiach Ben David or the Messiah from the house of David, a descendant of King David.

The reason for two is that there is to be separation between church and state. The High Priest has never been allowed to be King and the King cannot be the High Priest. Even back as far as Moses he was the leader, but Aaron was the priest. One must serve God the other serves the people as ruler and judge. Each is then able to devote all his energy to his duties and not have to divide his time. The priest can ensure that everyone

Apostasy of the Earthmen

knows God's laws and the King ensures these are obeyed, this is part of the problem today so many do not know what is right or what is wrong.

Our world is in rebellion against God, we deny the Bible, we contradict God's laws we promote cross dressing, transgenderism, and homosexuality. We either do not know or do not care and by denying the Bible we lose belief that the judgement that befell Sodom and Gomorrah really happened or that it could happen again. This is despite archaeological evidence showing that these cities were destroyed by a rain of brimstone, which is the ancient name for sulphur. Several YouTube channels have video showing evidence, but it is never included in education or mainstream programs.

The queer community claims that if you do not support them it is because you are not enlightened, but unfortunately for them they are the ignorant, both of history and the Bible. Society has lost the plot and it all begins with education, once religious studies were part of the school curriculum but today teaching religion, except for Islam, is banned in most schools. Our children have no idea where our laws came from or how our society grew, our history is painted as one of colonialism and racism and all the great developments are ignored. Society has devolved into a godless rabble, mostly uneducated or only taught a history that paints our ancestors as evil exploiters.

Apostasy of the Earthmen

What the propagators of this culture ignore is that without the capitalism and colonialism of the past we would still be living lives of subsistence farming and probably still falling prey to all those plagues that killed so many of our ancestors. Development of science and medicine takes a society that can afford to finance this research and development. Many civilisations have been around far longer than ours and developed so little. It is not because those races were inferior, but they never developed a culture of improvement. Western civilisation originally established this pattern of research and learning through the churches, even though some in the church fought against new concepts, the Pope jailed Galileo. It was religion based on the Bible, the religion on which we are now turning our back, that made us successful, I doubt that we can continue to be successful without it."

Apostasy of the Earthmen

Chapter 12

The summary of my view had obviously given the guests some food for thought and I hoped a realisation of why anarchy was gripping so many countries around the world. It was unclear whether their view had changed but the fact that they had returned was a good sign. Nor had they left or become bored with the discussion, which I felt was becoming a little like a lecture, they may become a group who avoided extremism. It was then that a recent member of the group asked, "If God controls the whole world why does he allow climate change and the destruction of the environment?"

I realised this was a guest who had been following the rhetoric of recent years and was concerned that the world would end through the climate effect caused by humans, so I was cautious with my reply. "The first thing to remember is that climate does change, the past has been both warmer and cooler than today. Life goes on species die others survive and improve. To believe that humans are responsible for everything is the epitome of arrogance we do not have that much control over the planet.

Since we abandoned the Bible and God, we think that we are above all else, that there is no supreme being who has oversight over all creation. That is our biggest error, we do not believe in God and we do not trust that he could control or repair nature. We convince ourselves that only we could be responsible and only we can fix it.

Apostasy of the Earthmen

I sometimes wonder if this is in response to the ancient prophecy that the world will be destroyed by the actions of its inhabitants. It is not driving SUV's or burning coal that will destroy the Earth it is man's inability to coexist with his neighbour.

It will be war and violence and men killing each other that will lead to the final destruction. We are already seeing some of this in Asia, in the Middle East and in South America and it is getting worse daily. Civil unrest is breaking out in USA and in Europe and South America. Self interest groups hope to destroy countries to build the society that they desire. In every case these ideologies are socialist in nature promising a fair deal for all but always ending with the population living in poverty as poor serfs while an elite ruling class accrues incredible wealth.

Invariably once the land and means of production have become the property of "the state" which is just a euphemism for the ruling class production falls dramatically. Those entrusted with production have no incentive, they will be paid whether they produce or not they have no incentive to produce more or better products because their salary will remain at the same labour rate no matter what the outcome. Quotas will be set but there is no reason to exceed these or to produce a better product to encourage sales.

Every state that has tried socialism or communism has suffered the same fate. These systems sound particularly good on paper but when it comes to human beings, they need a reason to plant more crops, to gain better yields and to produce products that are truly desirable. When incentive is missing so too is the need or encouragement to improve or increase production and eventually everything winds down and shortages begin to appear.

People need to be free, to have their own land to cultivate and produce. Their own businesses to manufacture or build to earn greater rewards for greater effort, people are not like insects slavishly working for the good of the hive or the nest, humans have a thinking intelligent mind which must be fully utilised to succeed, that is the Creators plan. To do less is to set the community into a spiral of decay and collapse, but man also needs to nurture his spiritual side or that too will decay into immorality and allow the deadly sins of lust, greed, sloth as well as sexual depravity to become the norm.

In the fifty-year period from 1967 until 2017 Western society underwent a collapse, interestingly this period coincided with Biblical Jubilee. It marked the time from when Israel regained its ancient capital of Jerusalem until the time that President Trump ratified that action by moving the United States Embassy from Tel Aviv to Jerusalem. The period began with the Egyptian Yasser Arafat forming the PLO and uniting the Arab residents of the area that Jordan had seized in 1948 and calling them "Palestinians"

Apostasy of the Earthmen

Palestine was the name given to Israel, Judea, and Samaria by the Romans when they drove the Jews from their homeland in 70 CE. The Romans chose that name as it was like the Philistines which was the name of a tribe of ancient pagan enemies of Israel. The modern Muslim inhabitants of Israel are predominantly of Arab, Syrian, or Egyptian origin. Some of the Muslims are also genetically Jewish, their ancestors chose to convert rather than flee or face death following the Islamic conquest of the Holy Land in 636 CE."

"The Palestinians are the descendants of the ancient Philistines, aren't they?" Inquired a guest, "No the original Philistines were destroyed a long time ago. Do you know the story of Samson and Delilah?" There was some nodding of heads and assent, so I continued, "When Delilah cut Samson's hair and weakened him the Philistines captured him and blinded him but during his captivity his hair grew back and he repented and prayed until his strength returned.

During the Philistines great festival in honour of their pagan deities they had decided to have some sport at Samson's expense and torture him to death. Unaware that his strength had returned they were having fun at the expense of their blind enemy. While they were all enjoying the festivities and making fun of Samson he found his way to the main pillars of their temple and although they thought it impossible for a man to move these pillars Samson moved them sufficiently to collapse the Temple at Gaza bringing down the whole structure killing himself and all the Philistines. Any Philistines who had not been at the festival were later dispatched by angry Israelite soldiers.

The thing that we have forgotten about the Bible is that the land of Israel is the property of the God of Israel. The Jewish people are simply entrusted with taking care of the land. When the Jews were driven out the land became a wasteland of deserts and swamps and was plagued by malaria. When the Jews began to return in 1867 and drained the swamps to create farmland and irrigate the deserts the mosquitoes diminished, and malaria was no longer a problem. When the land became productive Arabs began to come for work and later began to build on any vacant land.

There are photographs online of Joseph's Tomb, in the early 1900's it was standing alone surrounded by fields. Today it is in the middle of an exceptionally large Arab village the local Arabs have tried to destroy it several times, but the Israelis restore it and protect it. Jewish visitation is today severely restricted and soldiers guard visitors. Bethlehem was originally a Jewish town, and many Christians came to live there for obvious reasons.

Today it is an Arab town the violence of the Muslim Arabs has driven away all the Christians and Jews, the residents today make a living selling souvenirs to Christian pilgrims, but when they occupied the Church of the Nativity they used the part where Jesus' manger was believed to have been as a toilet. The Muslims have no respect for any other culture, the Koran encourages them to harass and kill "infidels" and to destroy artifacts that are not Islamic."

Apostasy of the Earthmen

Chapter 13

The guests were silent for a few minutes as I sat back and waited to see if there was any response. A little murmuring and side discussions were going on but apparently my concept was understood. It was then that a guest asked, "Do you need to be able to read Hebrew to see the hidden messages in the Bible?"

"To see the equidistant letter skips yes but there are many layers to the Bible and even just following the names and their meanings can reveal hidden messages. Take for example the first generations in the Bible. The first man was Adam, after Cain slew Abel Adam's next son was Seth, who was the father of Enosh. Enosh was the father of Cainan, who was the father of Mahalalel, who in turn was the father of Jared. Then came Enoch, then Methuselah, Lamech and Noah. The first ten generations of the Bible.

People sometimes wonder why the Bible has lists of names such as Adam begat Seth who begat Enosh and so on and wonder why the Bible makes these long lists but if we look at the meanings of the names we read another message. Looking at this first ten we see Adam means Man, Seth means Appointed and Enosh means Mortal. Cainan means Sorrow and if you have been listening to the meanings you might already realise there is a sentence forming.

Mahalalel means the Blessed of God and Jared means shall come down; Enoch means teaching. Methuselah

Apostasy of the Earthmen

means His death shall bring and Lamech means The Despairing and Noah means Comfort. We can see that all these names make up a sentence you can find the sentence simply by looking up the meaning of each name.

Now by reading just the meaning of each name and leaving out the name and the begetting we have a message that reads, "Man appointed mortal sorrow the Blessed of God shall come down teaching his death shall bring the despairing comfort." Many Christian Bible scholars jump at this as evidence that Jesus was the Messiah but if as I said earlier, he came as a sacrifice for our sins the "Lamb of God" does not necessarily mean Messiah. It would be nice if God does accept his sacrifice, but it still does not absolve people from following the law and not just the law of the land but Biblical law.

The interpretation does imply the death of a teacher or Rabbi, which means teacher. There have been many who have brought comfort to those in despair and many who have brought comfort even in death. It is undeniable that the names do make sense when read even if we cannot be sure of what that message says. It is just evidence that the Bible was compiled with greater knowledge and wisdom than humans possess."

I paused to see if there were any further questions or comments and another guest asked, "Do all Hebrew names have a meaning?" "Yes, in fact most names even

Apostasy of the Earthmen

English names have meaning there are a lot of books to suggest names for babies that give the meanings of names." "Does your name have a meaning?" "Yes, Tzemach means a branch or a plant, Ben means son and Alon means oak. I suppose if your Father's name means oak you are bound to be called a branch. My name therefore means the branch son of the oak."

"Is your name a Biblical name is it mentioned in the Bible?" "Yes, my name is mentioned in the Bible in Zechariah 3:8 … behold I bring forth my servant the branch. It is the only place I know of that it appears." "Why does it say bring forth his servant the branch is this something that someone named Tzemach must do?" "I don't know because I do not have insight to any special messages or directions from the Almighty to explain how I might serve; I may well not be the servant God is seeking. The children of Israel were redeemed from Egypt to serve God, so whether it is me or someone else of the same name only time will tell.

I think here we can take a lesson from the story of Esther; we may not even know what God wants us to do but if we do the right thing whatever he wants will be achieved. You should all take the time to read the story or look up the movie I think you will find it on YouTube and can watch it for free. Remember also that the Romans, the Ottoman Rulers, Charles Warren and Mark Twain all fulfilled prophecies without even being aware they had and without intending to be messengers."

Apostasy of the Earthmen

Another guest interrupted, "Are you saying that although you look like the end time guy described by Daniel and have the same name as the servant predicted by Zechariah that is all just coincidence?" "As far as I know yes, it may turn out that the Almighty has a plan for me but as yet I have no idea what it might be I guess I will find out when the time comes." "Then having a near death experience and seeing God and seeing or having a vision of Jesus are just coincidences?" "Maybe not but I cannot say because at this time I do not know.

Christian theologians sometimes claim the reference to a servant known as "the branch" means Jesus, even though his name means salvation. Which means that despite my name it could have nothing to do with me. Some theologians claim everything refers to Jesus. They read a lot of things into the comments and lessons of the prophets to support their view of Jesus as the Messiah or that Jesus is God, but who now sits at God's right hand in Heaven. To me much of Christian theology seems a little confused; just read the scriptures and do not try to fit them to your own ideas. I have seen nothing in the words of Jesus that is not a Jewish concept.

In fact, when Jesus was asked what was, "the most important commandment", he recited a line from the Shema, the prayer observant Jews say every morning and every night. That is, "You shall love the Lord your God with all your heart, with all your soul and with all you possess." I do not write off the possibility of a further role for Jesus, or any of us, I try to keep an open mind and not be blinded by opinion, either Christian or Jewish. The fact that Jesus has not fulfilled the events ascribed to be completed by the Messiah does not preclude God from sending him back to complete the job. Many Jewish people will be nervous to think that there could be a Christian King of the world as predicted by Nostradamus as Jewish experiences with Christian kings has not been good.

Even the "Good King Wenceslas" of the Christmas Carol was not particularly good to Jews, a fact of which most Christians are oblivious. Catholic countries are often inundated with Jew hatred that came from the old Roman Empire. Much of Europe was known as the Holy Roman Empire and was ruled by Rome through the church which moved away from Biblical teaching to a more Roman paradigm. Jews were considered a rebellious group who had to be defeated by Tiberius to bring peace to the Empire, that attitude has continued for centuries."

I had been talking for a long time and so stopped and asked if they wanted to continue today or should we come back next week and discuss some other topics. "I would like to hear more about prophecy, especially since you have had dreams and visions." Said one guest and several others nodded in agreement. "That is a big topic and could take a long time so I think we should make another time, or we might be here until breakfast." It was agreed after some minutes that we should book the venue again and so after a time and date for the next meeting were confirmed the group started to say their goodbyes and leave in small groups or singly.

Apostasy of the Earthmen

Chapter 14

A little over a week later we were headed back to our usual spot. The guests arrived individually and in ones and twos keeping their social distancing but with friendly greetings all around. In addition to hand sanitiser and the small sink by the bar in the private room I had taken the liberty of bringing in a traditional Jewish washing cup. When the guests had arrived and before ordering drinks or meals, I started the conversation by saying, "Did you know that washing the hands is a commandment?"

The question brought a few quizzical looks and so I said, "I told you there were six hundred and thirteen commandments in the Bible do you have any idea what they involve?" A little murmuring and some head shaking greeted this question and so I explained. "Apart from the obvious there are many quite mundane rules the ones that make news are those about adultery, drunkenness, homo sexuality and incest but there are also those about what food to eat and cleanliness.

In fact, it says that if a plague is in the land you should wash your hands and your feet in running water. There are two parts to the law, the written law, and the oral law the written of course is the part anybody can just read the oral law is more about how we do these things. Instead of writing many pages of instruction it is far easier to demonstrate." With that I used the washing cup to demonstrate washing the hands by pouring cups of water over each hand both front and back and explained. "It is no use simply wetting your hands and wiping them you must use sufficient water to ensure the hands are clean." The guests then took turns to practice the method I had just demonstrated, and I said, "This is why we have an oral law so that things like this can be demonstrated."

"Why does the commandment include washing the feet?" Enquired a guest, "In days of old people didn't wear shoes like we have today, they wore open sandals that collect dust and any dirt or bacteria that might be on the ground. Remember that many diseases like anthrax live in the dust and can be carried into the lungs by the wind. Therefore, livestock are particularly susceptible because they put their faces and noses close to the ground to eat. They can ingest the bacteria on the grass they eat or breathe it in as they graze, by washing the feet humans can avoid bringing bacteria into their homes."

After the washing, the drinks and meals were ordered, and we sat around the large table with first drinks and made small talk until the meals arrived. With the serving of the meals today I said blessings which they all observed. I wondered if it would become a habit with any of the guests or were, they simply curious in my presence. The conversation during the meal was quite light-hearted and a few questions were discussed from previous meetings making it apparent that some had been reading scriptures.

Apostasy of the Earthmen

A guest then asked, "What do you think of the Rapture, Tribulation, the Second Coming, and Judgement Day?" I replied, "Jewish beliefs about the End Times are based on the books of Ezekiel, Isaiah, Daniel, and Malachi as well as later rabbinic sources in the Talmud and Midrash. These traditions discuss key events that include: the Resurrection of the Dead, the Ingathering of the Exiles, the building of a Third Temple in Jerusalem, the reign of the Messiah our King, a descendant of King David

The relationship between these events and their timing are unclear, but several other factors will play a role. Elijah the Prophet, the "harbinger of the Messiah," is to return to anoint the Messiah. On Passover Jews set the table with an extra wine cup, the Elijah cup, it is predicted that Elijah will arrive for Passover but we at present do not know in which year. The Observant Jews do this every year so that they are always ready, just as some Christians try to live their lives as though Jesus could knock on their door tomorrow. Imagine it happened to you Elijah or Jesus arrived to announce the advent of Judgement Day would you feel confident or terrified.

The period immediately preceding the Messiah's return will be a time of great uncertainty and suffering. These "birth pangs of the Messiah" will include social upheavals. A great war will ensue between mighty nations as described by Ezekiel in his prophecy of Gog and Magog in Ezekiel 38 The end result will be a period of world peace "The wolf shall dwell with the lamb…" Isaiah 11:6.

The suffering and "birth pangs" the world is currently experiencing may well be the tribulation that Christians are expecting. Just as in the days Moses when he led the people out of Egypt there were miracles attributed to God, but the ten plagues visited upon Pharaoh and his people were natural phenomena. There was nothing that was supernatural or miraculous, but they came at the bidding of God. It is expected to be the same as we approach Judgement Day.

The prophecies say that the nations of the world will war against Israel and invade the land. God will bring them into the Valley of Jezreel and there he will contend with them. This is near the mountain of Megiddo, or Har Megiddo as it is called in Hebrew, it is from this place we get the term Armageddon. It is only at this time will anything remotely supernatural appear as the Almighty will cause terror among the invaders, their flesh will melt, and they will turn on each other.

The prophecies say the invaders will be successful for a time until God's Messenger also called the Angel from the East comes and declares victory for Israel. Not only do Biblical prophets predict a messenger from the East but so too does Nostradamus. He may have just been quoting the Bible, but he says, "Long awaited in Europe he will come from the deepest part of Asia." Implying from this that the awaited one is from South East Asia or

Apostasy of the Earthmen

Australasia. This would be a particularly good prediction for Nostradamus to make as Australasia had not even been discovered in Nostradamus' day."

"Isn't Australasia Australia?" Enquired a guest, "Well it includes Australia, New Guinea, Papua and New Zealand." I replied, "This means a messenger could come from our region. There is no indication that he is more than a mortal man or of any specific racial origin but the description in Daniel describes and him as old with white hair and beard. He may be the returning Elijah as predicted by Malachi, which would indicate an Israelite, therefore Jewish."

Another guest interjected, "Didn't you say one of the prophets said his name was the same as yours?" "Yes, that was in Zechariah 3:8, but it doesn't really mean anything unless something happens that I have to perform some task that puts me in the position of warning or advising people." "Isn't that what you are doing at the moment?" "Well I suppose in a way it is, and it might grow from talking to people like this, a part of that will be decided by what the people I talk with do afterward. The people who hear what I have to say or eventually write will either change their ways and become religious or discard it all and suffer any consequences. Jesus started off with only twelve followers but today his word has reached billions we all have the choice to inform or ignore, you choose."

Apostasy of the Earthmen

It was quiet for a moment and then another guest asked, "Does that mean we could all be involved in the events that lead to Judgement Day?" "Everyone will be involved whether for good or evil, it is up to you to decide. Our society has become an apostate society, denying the existence of God, and writing our own rules. China for example have camps to "re-educate" Muslims so they deny God, remember Muslims are mostly descended from Abraham's son Ishmael they are bound to God as much as the sons of Isaac, the Jews. Christians are also persecuted not so much in the west, but they are derided by the leftist globalists and people accuse religion of being the cause of all trouble."

At this statement, my original antagonist blushed, which I took as a good sign, he was now thinking about things before launching unfounded accusations, apparently realising that his original statement may have been ill advised. I continued, "The world is in a precarious situation at present. The leftists have managed to stop any religion being taught in the schools and this also extends to the history of religion which is an integral part of our history, because the founders of our society were religious and based our laws on Judeo/Christian values. The leftists who wish to control the world have removed this as just as George Orwell warned in his book "1984", whoever controls history controls the future.

By obliterating the past these globalists hope to create a new concept where the history taught will be that the society that existed before was evil and wrong. Which is why there is a push to destroy statues and monuments admired heroes set an example for people to follow. The new world order will be portrayed as wonderful and the only civilised way to live. The people will be brainwashed into believing this as we can see so many today already believe that owning things is evil and the world would be better if nobody owned anything. I have already spoken about the loss of incentive and how it impacts on production and quality.

Human beings were designed to compete and develop to find new and better ways to make better products and more food and improve quality and the quality of life. Just as we require exercise to keep our bodies healthy, we require challenges to keep our minds alert. To look for an easy way to do things or to be rewarded when not doing a good job discourages development and we become mediocre and gradually fall into a state of decline. Every socialist state that has ever existed has demonstrated this and as the population fails to learn or develop the leaders become ever more powerful, until they have no necessity of taking care of the population. These leaders become despots and invariably lead the people into a war as they look to expand their influence and direct the population's attention away from the decline. Starting a war effort also gives the population an incentive to work harder and better; to avoid being killed or conquered.

Democracies rarely start a war because people prefer to live in peace and prosper and an elected government starting a war is bound to find itself voted out of office. The only time an elected government needs to go to war is when the country is being attacked, a government that fails to protect its people is certain to be voted out of office. Dictators deliberately start wars to engender national pride in the populace and to supplement failing economies with the spoils of war. The Earth is currently in danger from several failing dictatorships such as North Korea, Iran, and China."

"But China is becoming the richest country on the planet," interjected one of the guests. "No," I replied, "China has manipulated its currency to flood the world with Chinese goods and has had many companies move their production to China for cheap labour and beneficial tax rates. They have created trade imbalances that enabled them to drain billions of dollars every year from western countries. Ever since Donald Trump became president, he has forced them into more equitable deals so that they cannot gain advantage. Following the Covid-19 outbreak many countries have realised how much they have become dependent on China's manipulation and are starting to restore their own manufacturing bases.

China have been buying iron ore from Australia and refining it into steel and then undercutting American producers to sell the steel. They use Australian coal to run the smelters but because they do everything on the cheap, they produce inferior quality steel. Australia would do better to smelt the iron themselves but the effort to stop using coal has taxed Australian producers into oblivion. Some of the iron ore and coal is used to make steel to build wind towers to satisfy the green ideology found in many parts of Australia. These are the biggest swindle of all, the amount of coal used to produce them will never be offset by the amount of electricity they produce. The value of power produced will never offset the cost of the towers, without taxpayer subsidies these would never be built, they are not profitable, either in power produced or in greenhouse gasses saved.

The Chinese economy is struggling the cost of building an army and navy to rival America and to establish their own space program has been a tremendous drain. Chinese companies have used fake bullion as security in some contracts. In only about twenty years they have tried to catch up with what America built up over almost one hundred years of investment. This rush to fulfill grandiose schemes has created a national debt the equal of the USA without the earning potential of America, particularly or comparable development. Much of their technology is learned, copied, or stolen from other countries, they have not taken the time to develop their own science. Now that they are being challenged over pirated intellectual property things are becoming ever more difficult.

All of these dictatorships have been guilty of imprisoning foreign nationals on falsified charges, simply to use them as bargaining chips in negotiations.

Apostasy of the Earthmen

The USA under President Trump has been increasingly successful in obtaining the release of a number of these hostages although some have come back in extremely poor health and even subsequently died. This is not a political battle this is a battle of good and evil, countries which have no religion have no moral compass. They feel no need to worry about the life or death of their citizens and even less concern over foreign nationals. It is this behaviour which will result in a final conflict as predicted in the Bible a war of annihilation for the forces of evil when the hand of the Almighty demonstrates karma, and all are judged.

The worst problem is that this attitude is no longer simply the domain of dictatorships, it has become the mantra for leftists, globalists, and even Green groups as they try to bring down free democracies. The attitude has also seen churches and synagogues attacked as part of the history they feel must be eliminated. The Karl Marx claim that "Religion is the opiate of the masses" has gained traction among these atheistic groups as they try to deny the existence of a Creator and portray the universe as an accidental coming together of atoms and molecules. Denying the principles of entropy these organised themselves into stars, planets and eventually life. A theory that flies in the face of scientific principles but which they claim is a more scientific theory than to consider intelligent design."

Apostasy of the Earthmen

Apostasy of the Earthmen

Chapter 15

The group was quiet for a few minutes then a guest asked, "If Muslims and Jews are bound to God through Abraham what about Christians?" "Through Baptism, and Communion, Christians bind themselves to Jesus as part of the "Body of Christ" not his physical body but the body or throng of those redeemed by his actions, and through those bonds also bound to God. Just like the other religions though they will also be judged by their good deeds. God is God he has no religion; he accepts all good people."

The conversation lulled for a few minutes and then a guest asked the grandfather of all questions, "If the Jews are God's chosen people why are they so hated? Why is there so much Anti-Semitism?" It took me a few minutes to think about this age-old question but then I realised I would need to go back to the early days. "Some of this relates back to the tents of Abraham, of the two sons God said the elder would serve the younger. The two sons accepted this but in later generations jealousies have arisen.

The Hebrews as a race were described by God as a "stiff-necked people" or stubborn but if you want someone to protect and remain steadfast to your word you must choose someone stubborn. The Hebrews even argued and bargained with God as long ago as Abraham who tried to save any "good men" who may be in Sodom and Gomorrah. God agreed to save the cities if Abraham could find good men in the cities, but eventually settled for sending two angels to save Abraham's nephew Lot and his family. The Sodomites showed their true colours in front of the angels and were sent blind for their efforts before being destroyed the next day.

In the days of Moses, the Hebrews tested God on so many occasions that God threatened to do away with the entire tribe. Moses pleaded with God to relent, not for the sake of the B'nai Israel but for the sake of the Almighty himself who had already invested so much in these people. Eventually the people divided themselves into two groups, those who would follow God's word and those who thought building a Golden Calf was a good idea."

A guest interjected at this point and asked, "Is there something significant about a Golden Calf?" "The Golden Calf was related to the worship of Baal who was glorified by the sacrifice of children. In those days there was no abortion you waited until the baby was born and you could sacrifice it to Baal by throwing it in the fire in front of the idol. These things were not unknown or even uncommon in pagan societies the Greeks left unwanted children, usually girls, in the forest for the Gods or the wild animals, whoever claimed them first.

The Romans just threw unwanted children in the sewer, it was only after the Torah was given and proclaimed all life sacred that people actually began to accept children as a blessing from God. Unfortunately, we have reverted to the time when the disposal of babies was seen as a normal practice, some people even insist on the right to "abort" a baby even if it is born alive. They refuse to see this as murder. As the world becomes more apostate and turns its back on God's laws life loses all value, even the elderly are aided to commit suicide because they no longer value their life and their life is not valued by those around them. People claim that this is because it is not living to suffer in pain but with modern drugs nobody suffers in great pain. We can get to a point where the level of pain medication can be just as lethal as the disease but that is different to wilfully ending life more often than not because of medical costs and financial reasons.

The importance of Baal being represented as a Golden Calf may go back to the story of Zeus who was reputed to have had sex with a heifer, I am sure a particularly attractive one." This elicited a few chuckles and giggles. "And sired a Golden Calf, the old pagan beliefs were all very intertwined. There may have been some elements relating back to the legends of a war in heaven, fallen angels and battles before God remade the world for us.

Even when arriving at the Promised Land the Hebrews who had seen all the miracles that brought them out of slavery in Egypt did not have sufficient faith to enter the land. They sent in spies to check out the land and the spies reported back that the land was populated by giants and said, "We were like grasshoppers in their eyes." The people hesitated forty days and then God sent them to wander in the desert saying, "I will give you a year for a day, you shall remain in the wilderness until all this generation shall pass away."

That was what led to the forty years of wandering in the wilderness. It was God's displeasure that there were still Hebrews who should have known of his power who had not enough faith to follow his word without question. In all societies there are weak and strong there are those who are wise and those who are not so wise. It is true of all races but for some reason especially among B'nai Israel.

Even today Jews can be divided into those who are faithful to Torah and practice their faith diligently and those who are Jews in name only. Some actively work against Israel and deny their heritage others flock to Israel as part of the ingathering and work to make Israel the garden that God intended. It is most obvious in the USA where the most pro-Israel President ever is taking great steps to aid the land to be what God intended and many of those arraigned against him are Jewish. Particularly among the Hollywood elite.

Hollywood is one of the world's leading centres of the push turning the Earth apostate and against God. They remake and distort old movies that followed the Biblical story. They promote homosexuality and gender confusion and they aim much of it at young children. This is not the example God intended for the Jewish people when he instructed them to be, "A light among the nations."

Many of the non-religious Jews are very left wing and even communist. This is what Hitler claimed in his book "Mein Kampf" the reason he gave for hating Jews was that they are all communists. He based this theory on the fact that Karl Marx was born Jewish but because of the restrictions on Jews in Germany his Father became Lutheran and Karl was baptised but later became an atheist. When the communists took over in Russia of the first thirteen members of the Politburo six were Jews. Re-enforcing Hitlers view that non-religious Jews were communists.

The descendants of Jacob appear to have an ability to choose either very well or very poorly. Just as Jacob was enthusiastic about God, his heritage, and industrious his brother Esau cared so little, he sold his birthright for a bowl of stew. Today many Jews are still choosing just as unwisely and are ignoring their heritage, often for wealth and fame and material gain. They are prepared to sell their immortal soul to gain wealth and fame and attack those who follow the moral Biblical instructions, possibly because they realise the good and moral people make them look bad despite their wealth and luxury.

Giving up your heritage to follow a Golden Calf is never a good idea, but many are willing to do it and urge thousands of others to follow suit. The denial of God, the Bible and the heritage that made men good and free and prosperous has created an apostate planet doomed to wind down to a final conflict that will destroy two thirds of the people in the world. God has said in both Isaiah and Zechariah that he would wipe man from the face of the Earth. Zechariah 13:8 And in all the land, declares the LORD, two-thirds will be cut off and perish, but a third will be left in it. 13:9 This third I will bring through the fire; I will refine them like silver and test them like gold. They will call on My name, and I will answer them. I will say, 'They are My people,' and they will say, 'The LORD is our God.'"

This may well be the tribulation that many Christian churches teach. Whether it is or not we are apparently in for some turbulent and testing time. The concerning thing is that we are right in the midst of these end time events." Having spoken for a good while I suggested it might be time to take a break and the group agreed, either getting up to move around or discussing one point or another with their friends.

Apostasy of the Earthmen

Chapter 16

The discussion had been going on for a while and I thought the group might be ready to call it a day when the instigator of the showdown stood up and addressed me. "When I challenged you I thought that religion was a crazy myth and caused people to go nuts, the trouble is that now I can see there is something in it and I can see what the world is turning into without guidance. You have scared the daylights out of us all and we do not want to be in the two-thirds of the population that gets wiped out, what should we be doing?"

"Fortunately, as well as the bad news the Bible provides good news it describes two things, the first is if you seek life observe the law. That is repeated several times throughout the Bible, from the books of Moses, the prophets and right up to the gospel. The second thing is to pray, I find it interesting that a couple of years ago Pew Research did a survey among Western Cultures, they found that only about one third were religious and prayed every day. It seems coincidental that the percentage of people who pray every day is the same as the percentage the Bible says will be saved.

You may have seen pictures of Observant Jews with their Kippah and Tallis and maybe even Tefillim, little boxes bound to their forehead and arm and reading from a prayer book. The prayer book is called the Siddur, which in Hebrew means order because it is the order of prayers. The prayers of those Jews call on the Almighty

Apostasy of the Earthmen

to "Extend your kindness to those who know you and your charity to the upright of heart." They ask God's goodness to be extended to all good people also included each day is a prayer that God will, "open your hand and satisfy the desire of every living thing." The Torah allocates responsibilities to all groups of people and to all freeborn, male Jews it allocates responsibilities not required of others to create the world that God wants, according to his word.

Women are not obligated to these time dependent prayers and obligations as, because of their nurturing instinct they have always been the guardians of tradition, molders of character, children, and family. Women have often been the protectors and the voice of reason when the natural aggression and impetuosity of the men may well lead the people into error or conflict. Women can and should be a calming and moderating influence on society but as women today strive to be more like men this balance is often lost. A lot of conflict today is driven by women who are no longer lady like.

The responsibility to pray for the welfare of others is only assigned to the Jews, the descendants of those who stood before God's Holy Mountain and to whom he spoke directly. I will say a little more about that when I come to discuss the law. Prayer is incumbent on all good people and I will first discuss the Jewish prayers as these are where all prayer developed. Cain and Abel made offerings to God and it was because Cain thought God respected Abel's offering more than his own, he became jealous and rose up and slew his brother. Prayers or offerings to God should not be the cause of dispute or jealousy. All should approach prayer as a holy and private thing between a person and the Almighty, He will decide who is worthy and approaches with piety and we should not worry about whether or not someone else is praying better or more often.

In fact, this is an area in which I believe Jesus was very right when he says in Matthew 6:4 so that your giving may be in secret. And your Father, who sees what is done in secret, will reward you. 6:5 And when you pray do not be like the hypocrites. For they love standing in the synagogues and on the street corners to be seen by men. Truly I tell you they already have their reward. 6:6 But when you pray, go into your inner room, shut your door, and pray to your Father, who is unseen. And your Father, who sees what is done in secret, will reward you."

A guest interrupted at this point and asked, "But what about Muslims, they take over whole city blocks and pray?" I responded, "Public praying like this is not about prayer or religion it is a form of bullying and harassment. The Muslim groups are proclaiming that that the world and God are their own private possession no other religion is permitted. If Jesus is right, they have had their reward and no more is due to them, but we continue to do what is right and just and trust in God and justice.

Apostasy of the Earthmen

Now let us consider Jewish prayer and in particular the main Jewish prayer recited every evening and every morning this prayer is called the Shema, because the first words are "Shema Israel" in Hebrew it means "Hear 'O Israel" and is a call to pay attention. The next part of the first line is a declaration, "The Lord is our God, The Lord is One." This does not really just mean one God but one with all creation, the force that creates and sustains the universe.

The next statement is said in an undertone because it is not really part of the prayer but a blessing on our creator, "Blessed is the name of his glorious Kingdom for all eternity." The next line is the one that Jesus quoted when asked what was the most important commandment, "You should love the Lord your God, with all your heart, with all your soul and all you possess." Some translate it as all your strength but all we have is only loaned to us by God and when he pulls the pin on you there will be nothing you can keep. We owe him not only our physical strength but also our worldly possessions.

Then we recite our duties with regards to this prayer, "These matters which I command you today shall be upon your heart. Teach them thoroughly to your children and speak of them when you sit in your homes and when you walk up the way. When you retire and when you arise. Bind them as a sign upon your arm and let them be Tefillim (an ornament) between your eyes And write them upon the doorposts of your homes and upon your gates.

Apostasy of the Earthmen

This is why Jewish men at prayer are often seen with small boxes or phylacteries attached to their arms and forehead as an outward sign of the obligation to have God's law control what your hands do and remain at the forefront of your mind. Jewish homes also have a small object called a Mezuzah attached beside the front door it also has the law encased. Just like placing the blood on the door at Passover it signifies that in this home we observe the laws given to us by God.

You do not have to be Jewish to love God, so you may recite any prayer you find suitable, there are many listed in the Bible and you can also pray to God whatever you like. We are assured that he will answer all prayers, just do not be too upset if the answer is no. How many times do you think the question, "Lord won't you buy me a Mercedes Benz?" might have been asked?

There are many beautiful prayers in the Psalms as well as from prophets we can choose from anywhere or write our own. In Christian cultures of course the most recited prayer is the Lord's prayer that Jesus taught when a follower asked him, "Master teach us to pray." He directed it to "Our Father in Heaven" not to an idol or himself or anything material on this earth. The prayer then simply asks God to provide the necessities of life, "Our daily bread" and then it asks to be forgiven of our sins. The prayer finishes by acknowledging God as the supreme power and the glory for ever and ever. A simple prayer that seeks only what we need.

Apostasy of the Earthmen

In this and in his many other teachings Jesus demonstrated his Jewish culture, he also showed it in many of the actions he took and in his behaviour. There have been many attempts in recent years to claim Jesus as something other than what he was, the Palestinian Arabs claim he was Palestinian, but Palestine did not exist at the time of Jesus. The Philistines were destroyed before Jesus was born and the current Palestinian group was not formed until 1964 when the Egyptian Yasser Arafat formed the PLO. It was Arafat who created the myth of a Palestinian people in 1969, after the 1967 war in which Israel regained the territory invaded and occupied by Jordan in 1948.

Some also claim Jesus was a homosexual because he was supported by a group of twelve male disciples. This ridiculous claim shows a complete lack of knowledge of Judaism and the culture in which Jesus lived and taught. According to Biblical custom certain prayers must always be conducted in a Minyan, which is a group of at least ten adult male Jewish men. Jesus chose twelve because he then had at least ten but also one to represent each of the twelve tribes of Israel. It had everything to do with religious custom and nothing to do with sexual proclivity.

Despite some prayers requiring special conditions all personal prayers may be conducted by anyone at any time. The most propitious times for prayer are when you arise to thank the Almighty for another day of life and before you retire to thank him that you have successfully negotiated the rigours of the day and ask his protection through the night. It is also appropriate to say thanks for food and show that you appreciate the good things with which you have been blessed, even God likes to know you are grateful for the blessings he bestows. There are many additional reasons to pray for help or protection and many things for which we should give thanks, but many people often just take things for granted.

We are assured by the Bible that prayer will bring rewards, but we should not just pray for reward. Prayer may not seem to help suddenly but it does make you a better person. It can also make you happier because you learn to concentrate on your blessings rather than your problems, giving thanks is a way to concentrate on good things rather than troubles. The human mind is a wonderful thing the greater amount of good it sees the more it gravitates to good things."

Apostasy of the Earthmen

Chapter 17

Having talked for a while I suggested a break, I knew that they were interested in following up on the law and what they might need to know about judgement, so I did not offer to finish. Once a short rest break had been enjoyed, I said, "I think I already mentioned that there are six hundred and thirteen commandments in the Bible and when I told someone that a long time ago I was told. "I don't think I could obey that many." The thing is you are probably already obeying many of them without realising.

If you are not having sex with your parents or brother or sister, you are obeying them. If you are not having sex with your animals, you are obeying them, so many of the multitude of laws are what we might consider mundane or common sense, but their observance makes us good and kind human beings. Treating people fairly and honestly, giving true measure and value are what makes society civilised and this is all that God asks of us.

The Ten Commandments were handed directly from God to the people, in Deuteronomy chapter five it tells of when God spoke to the people face to face and they were afraid. They pleaded with Moses to intercede on their behalf as they felt it impossible to hear the voice of God and survive. Moses went up onto the mountain and received the Ten Commandments that have been the basis of Judeo/ Christian culture since that time.

Apostasy of the Earthmen

When we look at these commandments, we can see that they are in two parts and were written on two stone tablets. On the very first one God identifies himself as the God who rescued the people from slavery in Egypt and commands, you shall have no other God but me. Second is you shall not make any graven image of anything on the Earth and shall not bow down to them. Third you shall not take the name of the Lord your God in vain, that includes claiming to take someone's life in the name of religion. Fourth remember the Sabbath and keep it holy, the seventh day belongs to the Lord and it should be honoured to honour him. Fifth honour your Father and your Mother respect begins in the family if it is not there it will not go well for society.

These are our duties to God, but as society has become more apostate and the Godless and atheists have gained control society has become increasingly hostile, belligerent, and violent. The commandments were given to prevent this happening but as apostasy has grown people have denied God, turned their back on the Bible and made their own rules. The last five commandments are our duty to our fellow man.

The sixth is commit no murder, in English they often say do not kill, but the Bible and the law acknowledges that some crimes are so horrific that the perpetrator has forfeited his right to life. It is also permitted to take a life, as in battle or to save your life or the life of another. Seventh is do not commit adultery, eighth do not steal and ninth do not bear false witness, which of course means do not lie but also do not falsely accuse. The tenth is do not covet and this is important because the breaking of so many other commandments can come from this, if you desire that which belongs to another you may be tempted to lie, steal or kill to get it.

The main aim of all the laws is to ensure that society grows and flourishes. It can only function properly if people treat each other fairly in all their dealings. If people cheat and deal dishonestly, they might gain in the short term but society as a whole will suffer. The land will only flourish if everyone can grow and produce and receive their fair share, if some are losing because of the actions of others eventually the whole system will fail. The rioting and vandalism being seen in many places means that not only do the victims suffer but society as a whole loses.

This is part of the problem with many Western societies today. Large powerful companies control vast sums of money and enormous factories, some are owned by hundreds of small investors, but others are controlled by extremely wealthy individuals. There is no problem in being rich in fact the Almighty wants us to be successful and wealthy but with that comes great responsibility. Jesus warned his followers that it was easier for a camel to go through the eye of a needle than for a rich man to get into heaven. Wealth must come through honest dealing and never to the detriment of others.

Apostasy of the Earthmen

The Biblical patriarchs were often wealthy, through God's blessing, and hard work they also nurtured and supported many others. To pursue wealth for the sake of wealth is to lose perspective on what is good and right. To do what is good and right can often lead to great wealth, the best and most productive workers are always the ones who succeed and earn good salaries or make many sales. You should aim to do good things and be of service to others then you stand a good chance of becoming at least a little wealthy. Once you become wealthy you should always remember those who are less fortunate, not everyone is able to have your skills and abilities just as we are urged to leave the corners of our fields as food for the poor we should always try to be charitable.

Something to remember about the law, is that it is not just there to be followed slavishly, it is there to make life better for all people. Just as we have the written and oral Torah so too should we think about the spirit of the law. It should be our guide to how we live justly, with kindness and mercy. The law outlines principles that have no prescribed measure such as charity to the poor, offerings to God and the church, pilgrimage, acts of kindness and Bible study.

The principles whose fruits a person enjoys in this world but also remain intact in the world to come are the honour due to Father and Mother. Acts of kindness, early attendance at the house of study morning and evening, hospitality to guests, visiting the sick, providing for a bride, escorting the dead, absorption in prayer, bringing peace between man and his fellow and study of the Bible is equivalent to them all."

I paused at this time to see how they felt about such a long discussion and guest commented, "When you condense it down like that the whole list of laws is not too hard to observe." "That is the whole purpose of Bible study, first to understand how we know God is real and secondly to understand what he expects of us, only by this are we able to achieve successful lives."

There was a pause for a few moments, and I asked if they thought it worthwhile meeting again, we had been here a long time today, but nobody appeared bored or impatient to leave. Due to the length of today's meeting I suggested we should look at finishing and considering whether there was anything else left to be discussed. There was a short discussion and then a guest said, "I don't know about anybody else, but I would be interested in a discussion on the last days." As this was a long topic, I suggested I collect more information and some references, and we meet again. The entire group were eager for this discussion, so we booked the venue for at least one further meeting.

Apostasy of the Earthmen

Chapter 18

The following week we met as per usual and I was surprised to discover all the same faces, nobody had quit the group. I decided to start my talk with the book of Enoch as this is one of the earliest existing discussions of Judgement Day. The book of Enoch makes fascinating reading and as we approach the climax of history many of the books of the apocrypha have been re-released and are now available due to an upsurge of interest.

Enoch, according to the Bible, was a favourite of God; he was taken away to heaven and did not die on Earth. In his book, Enoch explains that he was shown all the mysteries of heaven and earth and the whole history of the Earth from creation until beyond judgement. The book is written in chapter and verse in the same manner as other Biblical works and the segment, which is of interest to this discussion, is called "The Apocalypse of Weeks". The term week as used here is interchangeable with the word seven as in the ancient Hebrew these words are the same and are the same as in the book of Daniel (9:24).

In the past scholars have tried to reconcile the weeks or sevens to particular periods but to no avail, some have proposed that the "weeks" might be periods of seven centuries or even seven generations. Others have suggested that they may be unequal periods each marked by a great event. The ancients placed great emphasis on astrological signs, and it may be that the sevens were intended to relate to astrological periods, if they relate to

Apostasy of the Earthmen

a particular comet or similar phenomena this would explain variations in the periods. Enoch describes Judgement day.

ENOCH
93:15 Following this in the tenth week in the seventh part, there will be the great eternal judgement, in which God shall execute vengeance amongst the angels.

93:16 The first heaven shall depart and pass away, and a new heaven shall appear, and the powers of the heavens shall give sevenfold light.

93:17 After that, there will be many weeks without number forever and all shall be in goodness and righteousness, and sin shall be no more forever.

In addition to hinting at when judgement will occur Enoch also describes what will happen, after the Lord has promised judgement Enoch is shown the following vision: -
ENOCH 46:1
And then I saw one, who had a head of days,
And his head was white like wool,
And with him was another being whose countenance had the appearance of a man.
And his face was full of graciousness, like one of the holy angels.

46:2 And I asked the angel who went with me and showed me all the hidden things, concerning the Son of Man.

Apostasy of the Earthmen

Who he was, whence he was, why he went with the head of days.

46:3 And he answered and said unto me.
"This is the Son of Man who hath righteousness,
 With whom dwelleth righteousness.
 And whom revealeth all the treasures of that which is hidden.
 Because the Lord of Spirits hath chosen him.
 And whose lot has pre-eminence
 Before the Lord of Spirits in uprightness forever."

Enoch refers to God as the Lord of the Spirits and the Son of man who has righteousness is obviously a reference to the Messiah. We now apparently have a third identity that Enoch calls the "Head of Days" and has a similar parallel in Daniel who in describing judgement day mentions one whom he calls "The Ancient of Days"

DANIEL 7:13
As I looked, thrones were set in place
and the Ancient of Days took his seat.
His clothing was as white as snow; the hair of his head
was white like wool
His throne was flaming like fire, *
and its wheels were all ablaze.

7:10 A river of fire was flowing, coming out from before him.
Thousands upon thousands attended him.

Apostasy of the Earthmen

Ten thousand times ten thousand stood before him.
The court was seated, and the books were opened.
7:13 In my vision at night I looked, and there before me was one like a son of man, coming with the clouds of heaven.
He approached the Ancient of Days and was led into his presence.

7:14 He was given authority, glory and sovereign power; all peoples, nations and men of every language worshipped him.

In the book of Daniel (Chapter 7), there is a description of events leading up to the end of the world. In his vision, Daniel describes four beasts, which are four kingdoms, in the fourth, there are ten kings and after them one who usurps three others, preaches against God and the Messiah and attacks Israel. He is victorious until:
-

DANIEL 7:22
... the Ancient of Days came and pronounced judgement in favour of the saints of the Most High and then time came when they possessed the kingdom.

The "Ancient of Days" or "Head of Days" and his description is similar in both Enoch and Daniel and are consistent with other predictions which indicate that a herald will appear to usher in Judgement Day and the coming of the Messiah. Muslims are awaiting the arrival of a Mahdi to announce the return of Christ, according to Norse legend Heimdall, the whitest of the Gods, will sound a horn to summon the Gods at the end of the world.

A number of other clues may be found in legend, scripture and prophecies, in the past important religious leaders have been leading normal lives until the time came to do God's work. Moses was the son of a slave, who after his exile from Egypt herded sheep and goats until it was time to lead the people out of bondage. David was a shepherd and Jesus was a carpenter, so that it is unlikely that the next leader will be a king, a priest or wealthy.

Nostradamus may also be giving us a clue to watch for in:

Quatrain X: 75
Long awaited he will not return in
Europe but will appear in deepest Asia.
One of the league issued from great Hermes
And he becomes the most powerful of kings in the Orient.

Some commentators have suggested that this might refer to the third anti-Christ, but such a person is unlikely to be "long awaited". Hermes Trismegistos (Hermes the Thrice Greatest) was the Greek name applied to the Egyptian God Thoth, the reputed author of Hermetic writings. The writings also called Hermetica are works of revelation on occult, theological and philosophical subjects. Hermes-Thoth was one of the Gods and prophets to whom men turned for divinely revealed wisdom. Hermes Trismegistos (not to be confused with Hermes, son of Zeus) may tie in with other Biblical prophecies and the recurrent theme of a herald whom various prophets suggest is either Gabriel, Michael or Elijah returned to help recognise the Messiah and to comfort the faithful during the tribulations which precede judgement.

The Nostradamus prediction of an awaited descendant of Hermes coming from deepest Asia may link with a prediction in Revelation that says that after a period of darkness and signs in the heavens, which cause men to conceal themselves in caves to hide from the wrath of God;

REVELATION 7:2
Then I saw another angel coming up from the East, having the seal of the living God.

The concept of an angel coming not down from heaven, or God, but from the east differs from the usual definitions, which could mean that it is a descendant of one who was previously considered a God or prophet rather than a heavenly angel. A writer of Hermetica who gains great power after the signs appear in the heavens. Revelation simply says, "the East", Nostradamus says, "deepest Asia" which in Middle Ages France could mean anywhere from India to Australasia (which had yet to be discovered). In the ancient texts' angels were often referred to as "ben Elohim" or sons of God and sometimes simply messengers of God.

Apostasy of the Earthmen

Judgement it appears may be predicted to come before the Messiah's arrival. Nostradamus prediction of one who is "long awaited in Europe" but who will come from "the deepest part of Asia" may refer to the same messenger. This may also relate to the prediction in Malachi 4:5 "Behold, I will send you Elijah the prophet before the coming of the great and dreadful day of the Lord;" In the New Testament Jesus indicated that John the Baptist was Elijah reincarnate, and that "they did not recognise him", could it be that Elijah (John) has again been reborn and is waiting to be recognised?

In Jewish tradition an extra cup is placed on the table at Passover because the belief is that Elijah will arrive at that time of year in preparation for the coming of the Messiah. The messenger should appear at Passover, but the arrival of the Messiah is expected to occur on the ninth of Av on the Hebrew calendar which comes about two months before the Jewish New Year making it approximately late July or early August. Apart from days or times of the year Biblical prophecy does not indicate when this might all happen; we are expected to live a life of such righteousness that it will not matter if Judgement happens tomorrow or in another millennium."

Apostasy of the Earthmen

Chapter 19

Ending my talk at that point seemed to leave some guests disappointed and one asked, "Is there any way to get an idea when this might happen?" I replied, "Predictions from non-Biblical prophets give some clues but I am wary of promoting particular dates from them although everything indicates that the time is very near, I will give you a few ideas but I am not going to state specific dates but there are sufficient indicators that we are now only months from the final events.

Many people are looking for a whole chain of events to happen before Judgement can arrive, but the Bible says it will come as a "flood" meaning many things happening awfully close together. The scriptures also say that God made it in six days he can destroy it in an hour. Bearing in mind that God has been known to give a year for a day the hour might actually be one twenty-fourth of a year or about two weeks. As to the when, I have already mentioned St Malachy who implies that it is in the lifetime of the current Pope.

Nostradamus who lived from 1503-1566 said all his prophecies would be fulfilled within five hundred years. One of his prophecies did predict the resurrection of the dead, so he expected that to happen before 2066. In his quatrain X 74 he wrote, "The year of the great seventh number accomplished, it will appear at the time of the great games of slaughter, not far from the great millennium, when the dead will come out of their graves.

Apostasy of the Earthmen

The reference to the great games of slaughter may well refer to an Olympic Games, which were originally celebrated with the slaughter of a thousand bulls. This would make this a particularly accurate prediction because there were no Olympic Games in Nostradamus' day the modern Olympics were only commenced more than three hundred years after his death. Not far from the great millennium implies soon after the year 2,000 and we would expect that to be within the first half dozen games after 2,000.

I initially thought it might have been possible that it was meant for 2020 but there were other predictions that had not been fulfilled. I was not able to imagine how we would see the predicted economic collapse, it seemed possible under President Obama, but President Trump turned around the American economy and slowed China's take over, making it seem that the prophecies had failed. Once the Covid-19 virus hit the economic downturn happened more rapidly than I could have imagined.

Many nations are aligning themselves against Israel and Iran has signed up to Chinese initiatives and joint development creating all the players predicted in Ezekiel's (chapters 38-39) war of Gog and Magog. This war leads to the final battle at Armageddon, which in Hebrew is Har Megiddo or the Mountain of Megiddo. In Joel it says I will gather all nations and bring them down to the Valley of Jehoshaphat. There I will put them on trial for what they did to my inheritance, my people

Apostasy of the Earthmen

Israel, because they scattered my people among the nations and divided up my land.

I will gather all the nations and bring them down to the Valley of Jehoshaphat.
There I will enter into judgment against them concerning My people, My inheritance, Israel, whom they have scattered among the nations, as they divided up My land. They cast lots for My people; they bartered a boy for a prostitute and sold a girl for wine to drink.

In Isaiah, For by fire and by His sword, the LORD will execute judgment on all flesh, and many will be slain by the LORD. "For I know their works and thoughts; the time is coming to gather all nations and tongues, and they will come and see My glory.

Also, in Joel, Let the nations be roused and advance into the Valley of Jehoshaphat, for there I will sit down to judge all the nations on every side. Multitudes, multitudes in the valley of decision! For the Day of the LORD is near in the valley of decision

In Micah 4:12 But they do not know the thoughts of the LORD or understand His plan: that He has gathered them like sheaves to the threshing floor.

Zephaniah 3:8-9 Therefore wait for Me," declares the LORD, "until the day I rise to testify. For My decision is to gather nations, to assemble kingdoms, to pour out upon them My indignation, all My burning anger. For all the earth will be consumed by the fire of My jealousy.

Apostasy of the Earthmen

For I will gather all the nations for battle against Jerusalem…

It is apparent from all these prophecies that although the time is short the nations have not yet been gathered against Israel. When a prophet arrives at Passover and an invasion of Israel begins, we will know it is nearly time. The prophecies assure us that Israel's victory will not be by force of arms but by the will of God. We do not know exactly what date, but I would not be surprised if it came at the time of the deferred 2020 Olympic Games. The ninth of Av falls just days before the planned new commencement date; July 2021 might turn out to be a remarkably interesting time."

Apostasy of the Earthmen

Chapter 20

The room was deathly silent the group seemed a little stunned that I had suggested the culmination of all prophecy could occur in little more than a year from today. It took a couple of minutes before one of the lady guests asked in quiet almost unsteady voice. "What is going to happen to us?" I looked her right in the eye and replied, "The same as everyone else on Earth, if you have led a good life and not been violent, dishonest or unjust to your family and neighbours you need have no fear, if you have done otherwise you should try to make restitution and seek forgiveness immediately. There is no escaping this just there is no escaping death."

Another guest then said, "It's alright for you, Jews are the chosen people." "Only chosen to serve God and to be light unto the nations, I am shining a little of that light on you now." "But we are only Gentiles what hope have we got?" "You have the same hope as everybody else, in Hebrew Gentiles just means "Nations" that is the nations that are not B'nai Yisroel, not the children of Israel. You do not have to be Jewish to love God and obey his laws."

"Why are Jews so different?" "Jews are not really different to other people we have good and bad, dumb and smart and nice or mean people just the same as every other race." "You can't deny that Jews are smarter than most other people, they have won more Nobel Prizes than any other race. So many famous scientists and doctors have been Jewish." "Well according to Jewish tradition when God spoke to Israel face to face, he changed all Jews for all time. It did not make sense for an exceptionally long time that such a patriarchal society should have a law that you were only Jewish if your Mother was Jewish. In these days with our understanding genetics we now realise that you only inherit your mitochondrial DNA from your Mother, if God did make changes to the people at his Holy Mountain those changes can only be handed down by the Mother.

This has meant that although Judaism seems sexist to some, it is this treasuring of the women that has been the formula for survival. Each person has specific duties the men must serve God and study and learn the scriptures while providing a living for the family. Men must also say the prayers at set times and be ready to assemble in a Minyan when required. Women are exempt from all these duties as their responsibilities to the family are equal to their duties to God. In the society in which we once lived this was the normal and accepted standard but the influence of leftist socialist dogma has changed our paradigm for all time, the communist agenda of eliminating religion and gender differences has made us an apostate planet with the majority of the population against God and just waiting for the reaping."

Apostasy of the Earthmen

Chapter 21

Again, there was a pause in the room and a guest asked, "Are you saying that socialism/communism are the anti-Christ?" "I do not know if I would say anti-Christ, I would say Anti-God and the Bible. Karl Marx although born Jewish became a Lutheran when his Father converted for political reasons and then he became an atheist. Marx said, "religion is the opiate of the masses," in other words he saw no value in religion and no possibility of the existence of God.

The Communist Manifesto written by Marx sets out the way for communist forces to take over the world, in 1963 the aims of the communists were written into the congressional record in the USA as a warning of these sinister Godless people and their intent for western society." I scrolled through my smart phone and Googled the page and then I read what was chronicled in the records of Congress.

"Congressional Record--Appendix, pp. A34-A35 January 10, 1963. Current Communist Goals

CURRENT COMMUNIST GOALS

1. U.S. acceptance of coexistence as the only alternative to atomic war.

2. U.S. willingness to capitulate in preference to engaging in atomic war.

3. Develop the illusion that total disarmament [by] the United States would be a demonstration of moral strength.

4. Permit free trade between all nations regardless of Communist affiliation and regardless of whether or not items could be used for war.

5. Extension of long-term loans to Russia and Soviet satellites.

6. Provide American aid to all nations regardless of Communist domination.

7. Grant recognition of Red China. Admission of Red China to the U.N.

8. Set up East and West Germany as separate states in spite of Khrushchev's promise in 1955 to settle the German question by free elections under supervision of the U.N.

9. Prolong the conferences to ban atomic tests because the United States has agreed to suspend tests as long as negotiations are in progress.

10. Allow all Soviet satellites individual representation in the U.N.

11. Promote the U.N. as the only hope for mankind. If its charter is rewritten, demand that it be set up as a one-world government with its own independent armed forces. (Some Communist leaders believe the world can be taken over as easily by the U.N. as by Moscow. Sometimes these two centres compete with each other as they are now doing in the Congo.)

12. Resist any attempt to outlaw the Communist Party.

13. Do away with all loyalty oaths.

14. Continue giving Russia access to the U.S. Patent Office.

15. Capture one or both of the political parties in the United States.

16. Use technical decisions of the courts to weaken basic American institutions by claiming their activities violate civil rights.

17. Get control of the schools. Use them as transmission belts for socialism and current Communist propaganda. Soften the curriculum. Get control of teachers' associations. Put the party line in textbooks.

18. Gain control of all student newspapers.

19. Use student riots to foment public protests against programs or organizations which are under Communist attack.

20. Infiltrate the press. Get control of book-review assignments, editorial writing, policymaking positions.

21. Gain control of key positions in radio, TV, and motion pictures.

22. Continue discrediting American culture by degrading all forms of artistic expression. An American Communist cell was told to "eliminate all good sculpture from parks and buildings, substitute shapeless, awkward and meaningless forms."

23. Control art critics and directors of art museums. "Our plan is to promote ugliness, repulsive, meaningless art."

24. Eliminate all laws governing obscenity by calling them "censorship" and a violation of free speech and free press.

25. Break down cultural standards of morality by promoting pornography and obscenity in books, magazines, motion pictures, radio, and TV.

26. Present homosexuality, degeneracy, and promiscuity as "normal, natural, healthy."

27. Infiltrate the churches and replace revealed religion with "social" religion. Discredit the Bible and emphasize the need for intellectual maturity which does not need a "religious crutch."

28. Eliminate prayer or any phase of religious expression in the schools on the ground that it violates the principle of "separation of church and state."

29. Discredit the American Constitution by calling it inadequate, old-fashioned, out of step with modern needs, a hindrance to cooperation between nations on a worldwide basis.

30. Discredit the American Founding Fathers. Present them as selfish aristocrats who had no concern for the "common man."

31. Belittle all forms of American culture and discourage the teaching of American history on the ground that it was only a minor part of the "big picture." Give more emphasis to Russian history since the Communists took over.

32. Support any socialist movement to give centralized control over any part of the culture-- education, social agencies, welfare programs, mental health clinics, etc.

33. Eliminate all laws or procedures which interfere with the operation of the Communist apparatus.

34. Eliminate the House Committee on Un-American Activities.

35. Discredit and eventually dismantle the FBI.

36. Infiltrate and gain control of more unions.

37. Infiltrate and gain control of big business.

38. Transfer some of the powers of arrest from the police to social agencies. Treat all behavioural problems as psychiatric disorders which no one but psychiatrists can understand [or treat].

39. Dominate the psychiatric profession and use mental health laws as a means of gaining coercive control over those who oppose Communist goals.

40. Discredit the family as an institution. Encourage promiscuity and easy divorce.

41. Emphasize the need to raise children away from the negative influence of parents. Attribute prejudices, mental blocks and retarding of children to suppressive influence of parents.

42. Create the impression that violence and insurrection are legitimate aspects of the

Apostasy of the Earthmen

American tradition; that students and special-interest groups should rise up and use ["] united force ["] to solve economic, political, or social problems.

43. Overthrow all colonial governments before native populations are ready for self-government.

44. Internationalize the Panama Canal.

45. Repeal the Connally reservation so the United States cannot prevent the World Court from seizing jurisdiction [over domestic problems. Give the World Court jurisdiction] over nations and individuals alike.

SOURCE: Skousen, W. Cleon. Naked Communist Salt Lake City, Utah: Ensign Publishing Co. C. 1961, 9th edition July 1961.

Call Number: HX 56 S55"

It was apparent that the guests now realised just how far the apostacy of communism had come and that it was taking control of the Earth and had perverted a large part of humanity. They were now able to see that what was happening in the world was in fact a battle between good and evil and that which had been proclaimed good was really evil and that good was being called evil just as the prophets had warned.

"In a recent interview, renowned Israeli Rabbi Daniel Asor warned of a globalist takeover happening as we speak. "If Hitler is the Third Reich, then the New World Order is the fourth Reich. It is Amalek's last meeting with us before the Messiah's arrival" he said. Warning of a one world government ruling the world, the rabbi cautions that in the Hebrew calendar year *"Taf Shin Pey Aleph* (September 2020 until September 2021) from *Tevet* (January-February) until *Elul* (August–September) those will be the 9 months where the New World Order rules.

Even the renowned Rabbi expects the communists to be successful for a time, until the arrival of the Messiah. The atheist communists have gained control over so many of our institutions, big business, education and media companies that most people have no idea what the truth is they see what is in the news on the television, even late night entertainment has been tuned into a hate fest against Christian values and to quote the Bible can lead to charges of hate speech. To all intents and purposes the evil ones have won, God is imprisoned if you speak up you may be attacked, fined, jailed and at the very least ridiculed and accused of racism and homophobia.

It is because they see leaders like President Trump with his support for Israel, Jews, and Christians as a

Apostasy of the Earthmen

roadblock to their domination that they hate him with a passion. It positively galls them to see leaders like the UK's Boris Johnson and Evangelical Christian, Australia's Scott Morrison elected to their positions because that shows that there is still sufficient support for law, order, and moral laws among the population that their victory is not complete. It is even worse for them that these leaders are stopping the spread of communism and control coming from China even though there are many politicians who have sold out to China for financial gain.

If Ezekiel's flying machine was to return to Earth today the "creatures" that Ezekiel witnessed would be sending back their report that the Earth had become an apostate planet. The majority of the population has turned their back on their Creator, they are more interested in the material things of the Earth and enjoying all kinds of sexual depravity that is now considered normal. They have no idea that they have a need for a moral and spiritual guide believing that whatever seems right in their own eyes is acceptable."

I paused here but then another guest asked, "You mentioned the name Amalek as someone in a last meeting before the Messiah?" "The original Amalek was a grandson of Jacob's brother Esau and his tribe carried out an unprovoked attack on the Children of Israel while they were travelling in the desert. God ordered that the Israelites must totally destroy the Amalekites. The name Amalek is used today to apply to any group with evil intent and destruction in their hearts, we are still expected to totally destroy this evil. The globalist, atheist New World Order is the manifestation of this evil"

The meeting having gone on for quite a while I suggested that we should maybe call it a day and as I felt we had probably covered most of what was happening it might be wise to wrap it up. Some were a little reluctant but had no further questions right now, so I suggested that they compile their questions for one more meeting and we see if there is any need to go further for answers. The group agreed and so relaxed and mingled drifting away in their usual groups.

Apostasy of the Earthmen

Chapter 22

The following week I arrived early, with no plan for what we might discuss and no idea of anything that we might not have covered. I had brought a couple of books with me that might be of interest and provide more information and guidance but would wait to see how the other guests felt, or if they wanted to discuss their own questions. I ordered an early cup of coffee and sat reading as guests started to arrive. There were greetings and small discussions going on and things were decidedly informal.

Once people had met and greeted and wine and meals were ordered the discussions moved to the table where it was more of a casual conversation about the various topics we had discussed over our previous meetings. Several small questions were raised and I was surprised at the different things people had gleaned from my talks but the questions were minor points and I was not the only one with answers this time which was a rewarding feeling, my efforts had not been wasted and these people were more open about the possibilities.

A guest then asked, "What about the people who say the Israelites were really African or black and that Europeans only portrayed them as white?" "Well the Bible doesn't talk about colour to any degree, God is not racist. The few mentions of colour mention Noah's son Ham who is described aa "dark" or possibly black. The other character whose colour is mentioned is Jacob's brother Esau who is described as red and hairy like a hairy garment. Natural red hair is not a common trait among dark skinned people and very dark people are rarely hairy. Esau's arms were so hairy that Jacob wrapped his arm in the skin of a kid to convince his blind Father that he was Esau.

A guest then turned and addressed me, "You know when I first came here, I thought it was all just old myths and legends, but you have made me realise that it could all be true. I tell you I am now scared that not only is it true but you might be right that we are going to see Armageddon any day and the thought that God is real and will be there is frightening." I replied, "That is a really good thing because the Bible says that the beginning of wisdom is the fear of the Lord. It demonstrates that you are gaining wisdom.

The thing to remember is that although the thought of meeting an all-powerful Creator of the universe is frightening, he is also like a loving Father and you should love him in return. He may be powerful, and he is certainly strict, but he is forgiving to those who love him. He understands the fallibility of the flesh, we must remember that a human being is made of two parts we grow from the dust of the Earth but are animated by the spirit that God breathed into us to give us life.

What are we, what can we say to our Creator the God of our Forefathers, all the heroes are like nothing before him, the famous as if they never existed, the wise as if devoid of wisdom and the perceptive as if devoid of intelligence? Most of their deeds are desolate and the days of their lives are empty before him. The pre-eminence of man over beast is not existent for all is vanity. In our prayers we ask for his mercy on all those who know him and for the upright of heart, this is what separates the spirit and his children from the dust of the earth. In gratitude for this gift we should thank him and praise him at least twice every day, evening and morning and say a blessing for the sustenance he provides and the countless other blessings we receive each day.

When we lose this sense of gratitude or think we have gained all these blessings purely on our own is when we begin to forget about God. We forget his laws and his ways we think there is nothing wrong with deviant sexual practices. We think violence bullying and terrorism are valid means to achieve our goals. We abandon the sanctity of life; we kill unwanted babies or the old and the ill because we think that life no longer really matters, we revert to being no more than the beasts. All that made us better is gone. Be grateful that you now have the wisdom to fear God.

There are a couple of important factors so often overlooked in life that cause so much trouble and heartache. The first is that we should be thankful for what we have and not worry about what we do not have the man who wants what he gets is happier than the man who gets what he wants. The second is that what happens to us in life is only ten percent of life how we react to it is ninety percent of it, if we are accepting and understand that things will not always be as we want we will not feel continually frustrated and unhappy.

Talking about being grateful for what we are given and appreciating all that we have reminds me of a story I heard from the time of the Holocaust. A Jewish man was standing out of sight from the guards and praying his friend stood near him and softly said, "What are you doing? It's too late for morning prayer and too early for afternoon prayer." The man replied, "I am just thanking God." "What have you got to thank him for you're in a concentration camp.?" "I am just thanking him that I am one of us and not one of them." Even if you are a victim and treated poorly you can still be grateful that you are alive and that you have not descended to the level of the beasts."

One of the guests then remarked, "A lot of religious thought is really philosophy isn't it?" "I think that's where philosophy began but because there are many who want to exclude God from life, they rewrote many of the concepts to try and be far more mechanical. It is this denial of a Supreme Being that has led to all the World's problems as we try to explain a world without God and where man is the ultimate decider of right and wrong. The denial of the Bible is an industry of the leftist, atheist agenda, even to the extent that archaeological evidence is suppressed and ignored. There are even books that present long drawn out explanations of how these stories were invented but they ignore the evidence, which even when new discoveries are made truly little mention is made by the mainstream media."

"What sort of recent archaeological discoveries have been made and not publicised?" Asked a guest, "Just recently near the new United States Embassy in Jerusalem they found a storage vault and in it were fragments and seals bearing the name of the Biblical King Hezekiah. This of course goes against the leftist narrative that the Jews do not belong in Israel, the writing on these seals not only has Biblical detail but is written in Hebrew proving the Jewish claim to the land since Biblical times.

The evidence that I think has been most carefully hidden is found further South and has been known for over fifty years. Have any of you heard of a place called Nuweiba?" Blank looks and shrugs greeted my question. "Nuweiba is a coastal town in the eastern part of Sinai Peninsula, Egypt. Located on the coast of the Gulf of Aqaba. The full name of the town in Arabic is Nuwayba'al Muzayyinah, which means "waters of Moses open," which should give you a clue as to what is interesting about this town.

In 1967 following the Six Day War Israel occupied the Sinai Peninsula but eventually returned it to Egypt in exchange for a peace treaty. It meant though for a time the area was opened up for tourism, following the peace treaty the Egyptian government is still encouraging tourism and I believe even opening new roads to generate income from tourists. Once the area was first opened Biblical scholars took their diving gear and went to see what was under the water. A number of videos have been shared on YouTube and social media showing the discoveries.

What these divers found were strange coral structures unlike those anywhere else in the world. These coral shapes have formed in the shape of Chariots and their wheels and axles. Obviously over the millennia the chariots themselves have decayed but the corals that grew on them hold their structure even today. These coral structures extend the whole width of the Gulf of Aqaba and can be seen off the shores on both the Egyptian and Arabian sides.

Even more interesting is that originally there were two red granite pillars each side of the crossing point and local legend claimed that these were erected by King Solomon only three hundred years after the sea had opened to allow the people to cross. The pillar on the Egyptian side is still there but has been moved back from the actual shoreline and the original Hebrew inscription has been removed. The pillar on the Arabian side has been completely removed and its existence or location is currently unknown.

In addition to this evidence there are, on the Arabian side the Mountains of Midian, one of which has a mysterious blackened top and at the foot of it is a stone altar on which is etched the figure of a bull. There is also a huge rock that has been split in two and from that there is evidence that a great volume of water poured out and down the hill. All these things are evidence of the biblical narrative of Moses leading the children of Israel from captivity, but nobody apart from a handful of archaeologists and Biblical scholars has any idea that any such proof exists.

Further evidence has very recently been found on the shore of the Red Sea on the coast of Egypt. The remains of a large army has been found only last year. Those who have examined the find believe there are as many as five thousand remains in the area. My own theory is that these remains have been carried down from Nuweiba, because scripture tells us that the sea was opened by a great wind, if the wind pushed the sea to the North end of the gulf once the wind stopped the water would return like a tsunami. Those caught in it would either be overturned and bogged where they were caught, or they could be carried for many miles until the water pressure dropped. This would explain why many from the pursuing army could have been trapped at Nuweiba but then carried back to Egypt's own shores.

The recent discovery was not publicised in any mainstream media and only carried by some religious journals and archaeological references. The religious news treated it with great excitement, but the archaeologists simply took it as a matter of curiosity. Apart from physicists very few scientists are able to discuss religion without attracting the ire of their peers, the atheist dogma has been so firmly instilled in our institutions and universities."

Apostasy of the Earthmen

Chapter 23

The room was incredibly quiet and then the organiser and instigator of the group, addressed everyone, "You know what this means people?" He had their attention and he continued, "Everything we have been taught in our lives is a lie, we have been misled by an atheistic conspiracy that has turned us into unthinking sheep following the crowd." He was obviously annoyed that there was information he should have been given the opportunity to examine, to decide for himself, but it had been hidden and derided as myth and legend.

I spoke up and said, "Do not worry about what has been done you cannot change the past, you may yet have the time to confirm all this for yourself, but even more importantly to help inform others. Even though if you start quoting the Bible on social media you will probably be blocked you will not even be able to speak out against, homosexuality, adultery, or any of the forbidden things mentioned. Even if you do not wind up suspended from your social media accounts you run a good chance of being fired from your job or sued by someone who feels offended because you believe their behaviour is unjust and immoral.

I have been writing that book that was suggested and I will get your email addresses so that when it is released you will be able to read it. What will be more important will be to find people who will discuss it, read it and urge others to do the same. Two thousand years ago

Apostasy of the Earthmen

Jesus spread his message around the world through word of mouth, with just a dozen supporters and no modern communication. I mention Jesus and not Moses because Moses had the entire tribe of Israel as witnesses who saw those events, Jesus had his disciples.

Naturally as an attendee at Synagogue and not a Christian church I study the Hebrew Bible and not necessarily the Gospel, although I have read it and I did notice that in 2 Timothy 3:1-5 there is a prophecy that appears very accurate in describing the world today, it says, "This know also, that in the last days perilous times shall come. For men shall be lovers of their own selves, covetous, boasters, proud, blasphemers, disobedient to parents, unthankful, unholy, Without natural affection, trucebreakers, false accusers, incontinent, fierce, despisers of those that are good, Traitors, heady, high-minded, lovers of pleasures more than lovers of God; Having a form of godliness, but denying the power thereof: from such turn away."

The world today has been shaped by the communist aims and those whom the communist hierarchy once referred to as "the useful idiots" who have been unknowingly indoctrinated by their educators and the mainstream media. All those communist goals that the US Congress was warned about in 1963 have been attained and the world has become an apostate planet, denying the very existence of God, except for a select few. The prophecies continue to be fulfilled and the people are behaving just as prophesied, when it was predicted that it would be just as in the days of Noah. They will continue on in their own evil ways until the catastrophe carries them away and they are no more.

People today do not even know about Sodom and Gomorrah and yet there is archaeological evidence that those towns were showered with burning sulphur, which in those days they called brimstone. In the ruins are still found pieces of unburned sulphur and evidence of people and goods burned in the fire. They refuse to believe that this really could have been a punishment for sin and insist that if it did happen it was just a natural disaster. The idea that a warning was given is met with disbelief just as the suggestion today that judgement awaits us all is greeted with derision.

It will come suddenly without warning the disbelieving will run to hide but it will do them no good. Those who call on the Almighty for his mercy will receive it, that is his promise and his guarantee. We were not created to be destroyed but are given the chance to become what we were meant to be, if we refuse that; and ignore God and what is right then we will perish. The denial of God and the disregard or in some cases the outright reversal of Biblical law has led to the chaos and violence that now controls so much of our society. Humanity has degenerated from a developing species aspiring to greater heights to an undisciplined rabble grasping like savages or animals and unless this is reversed the species is doomed.

Apostasy of the Earthmen

Unfortunately, in the battle between good and evil, the evil forces have won over most of the population. They can never see what is wrong because the denial of the Bible and God has blinded them, one who reads this and is unable to believe it has had his mind closed by the atheist leftist manipulation. We should try to encourage people to try to learn the truth for themselves but the more we try to convince the more determined many will be not to believe. Some will find it too terrifying to allow themselves to believe or even to find out more than what they have been told. It can be frightening to think that the world we know is about to end.

The financial collapse is upon us and the winds of war are blowing stronger every day. China and Iran are in dire financial straits and of course blame Western sanctions rather than face up to the fact that it was their own aggressive actions that forced those seeking peace and security to apply sanctions. Financial manipulation and unfair trading practices have enabled some groups to gain huge advantages over the honest traders until ever greater amounts have been concentrated into fewer hands and corrupt politicians have been party to much of this fraud. The result is that the people who simply wish to earn a living and support a family are those who suffer most in the end. Once these consumers are unable to buy their necessities the entire financial system collapses.

I have been discussing this in religious terms as a battle between good and evil or right and wrong. There are many who will not see it as anything but a conflict of political views. The fact that the events are following a prophesied course is lost on them they either cannot or will not see it because their minds are so focussed on the material world. Those who are able to recognise the signs should try to point them out and urge their associates to become aware of the truth behind what is happening. If you warn someone and he ignores it that is his fault, but if you do not warn him you may become complicit in his error.

The violence and anger of the left is borne by a frustration they feel because not everyone believes as they do, those who disagree are wrong and an enemy of the people. The attitude that anything other than socialism is criminal and religion is a drug for the masses and cannot possibly bring any good is so ingrained that they must violently resist any attempt at reason. A major part of this resistance is that because the arguments against their views are so sound, they have trouble refuting them with logic, violent abuse then becomes the only manner in which the leftists can respond. A major part of the problem is that they were convinced that socialism had been victorious, but the election of conservative, religion supporting leaders has shattered their dream."

A guest then said, "You don't like socialism much do you?" I replied, "It is a failed system, everywhere that it has been introduced has turned into a communist dictatorship and it has cost over a hundred million lives since communism first took hold in Russia little more than a century ago. Russia and China alone saw the deaths of over sixty-five million citizens. Venezuela was once the fourth most successful country in the world. They had great wealth from oil and industry as well as a very productive farming sector, once the socialists came to power people lost everything and now, they cannot even afford to feed their own population.

Seizing all private property in the name of the "state" does not help anyone to run a business or to provide goods and services that might be needed by his fellow man. When the means of production become the property of an artificial entity such as a state or government body the need to produce good quality product which is needed, no longer becomes a priority. Once all effort to obtain market share and produce marketable products ceases the sales fall away and the goods are no longer being sold. Once goods are not being sold it is pointless to produce them and so the whole industry fades into oblivion and the employees no longer have employment. Unfortunately, socialism begins a downward spiral that eventually leads to failure.

It begins with education because the whole aim of the communists was to take control of education and the media, which has happened. The first communist trained students are now the teachers, in a recent riot there were nearly two dozen arrests and about two thirds of those arrested were teachers. The Christians and conservatives have lost the battle, the atheists and communists are now teaching the children and controlling the narrative. The battle between good and evil has been won except for the prophecies. The world will be stunned when the final events unfold because nobody believes it possible."

Apostasy of the Earthmen

Chapter 24

I paused at this point realising I had covered quite a course over several weeks. Commencing with just a discussion on why religion was not the cause of Earth's problems to a conclusion that the lack of religion brought about by communist doctrine was what was driving the violence and trouble now consuming such a large part of the civilised world. There was no way to know if the guests who had been coming each week to listen had in fact decided that my conclusions were right or whether they would go away and shrug the whole episode off as an interesting but unremarkable idea..

In the beginning I had no intention of taking the conversation this far, I had never envisioned being able to explain to this group of people with no religious knowledge the enormity of the forces that were now drawing humanity to a final destination that had been foretold millennia before today. I had also revealed more of my personal experiences than I had intended but it had seemed the thing to do at the time.

The value of telling these people all this information was impossible to assess, but I hoped that it would help them at least, to understand things that are happening in the world today. I explained, "Biblical scholars are noticing a pattern to events, but the majority of people are continuing on blissfully unaware that anything is happening or just wondering why the world is as it is. To the Biblical scholar it is apparent, we cannot but believe the world is moving to its final epic battle between good and evil. The fact that today so many people question which is which is proof that the battle is almost lost, but even the very evil suspect that their time is short, and they may be found wanting. The violence and fanaticism that drives the riots and rebellion today is a symbol of their desperation.

Those of us who know the Bible and prophecy must try to educate those who are looking for answers but we know that to try and inform the wrong people will result in violence, aggression or even law suits as Biblical quotes are often labelled hate speech. We can do nothing more than warn the world and hope that some might be saved who would otherwise be doomed."

The guests sat quietly for a minute and then one asked, "If there is only a short time until all this happens, what can we do?" "There is nothing you can do to stop it, just like death or an asteroid striking the Earth it will happen at its prescribed time. I doubt whether we can influence enough people to make the result any better. There are however things we can do to make our own situation better. The world has lost all perspective because the inhabitants of the Earth have turned their back on God, often denying his very existence.

We can see the result all around us, people's priorities are all wrong. The young think nothing of spending more on tattoos than on their teeth, they buy trendy brands even though they know many of these are made in sweat shops with what amounts to slave labour. Many live a life of crime rather than gaining an education and becoming productive members of society. The socialist paradigm has been taught in schools until the young feel that all employers are exploiters and there is no honest road to success."

Another guest spoke up and said, "It all sounds very sad and disheartening." I replied, "It is, I am old enough to remember the excitement and optimism for the future that society enjoyed in the late 1940's and through the 1950's the war was won and despite the rise of communism in Russia and China the rest of the world was rebuilding and optimistic about the future. The paradigm that our society was evil and built on the backs of slavery and colonisation and our forefathers were evil, has only been created by the atheists and the communists who set out to destroy our history, our religious beliefs and our society.

In the US Constitution it states facts that are what they call self-evident, but those principles are Biblical attitudes that are against the plan of the deniers of Biblical truth. We should remember many things for example the Bible recommends a "wine libation" as a means to sanctify a meal but speaks volumes against drunkenness, if you are unable to stop at two drinks then do not drink. Even Jesus recommended wine and bread and turned water into wine many cultures have a tradition of enjoying a regular glass of wine or as we say in Hebrew a cup of kiddush, which means sanctification.

Apostasy of the Earthmen

There is a legend about the discovery of alcohol that I believe everyone should learn. It claims that many eons ago a worker was bringing the produce from his master's vineyard to the town when he noticed one of the packs on a donkey was leaking. Not wanting to bring in less than he started with he looked for something in which to collect the leaking grape juice, and he found the skull of an eagle. It was only a short time later when this was full, he had to find something else and he found the skull of a lion. Continuing on before he reached his destination that too was full, so he looked for another receptacle and was fortunate to find the skull of an ass.

According to the legend that is why the first glass of wine gives one the vision of an eagle, the second will grant the courage of a lion but the third brings the stupidity of an ass. It is traditional in some cultures to drink a little extra at times of celebration but at all times retain decorum and good standards of manners. Unfortunately, today many people indulge in binge drinking and lose all inhibitions and behave in quite unbecoming ways. The lack of proper education and moral instruction leaves people unable to prioritise their lives to achieve anything worthwhile.

When people do not understand what is sensible or even moral, they make bad choices, they wonder why their lives seem to be permanently difficult yet continue to do the same wrong things. It is a little like gambling without realising that there is always a house percentage, bookmakers and lotteries do not run these things to make other people rich. I have no problem with occasionally buying a raffle ticket if the proceeds are going to a good cause, I do not buy it in the expectation of winning but as a means to contribute. In the event I did win a prize that would be a bonus, in life we do not gain anything for nothing. If the Almighty feels that we are worthy of a reward we will receive it, if someone else gains the reward I assume that God felt he was more worthy."

Apostasy of the Earthmen

Chapter 25

I paused at this time to see if the guests were satisfied or had further questions, and guest asked, "You seem so sure of Biblical prophecy do you just take it from what you read in the Bible or do you think there is other tangible evidence?" I responded, "There is definitely further evidence, but it is never reported in the mainstream media because it goes against the leftist atheist paradigm and even if they hear it, they deny the possibility. The first Prime Minister of Israel, David Ben Gurion summed it up when he said, "In Israel, in order to be a realist, you must believe in miracles. Many of the normal and regular happenings in Israel would be strange and miraculous according to peoples of other countries."

There are actually videos posted on YouTube that show some of these modern miracles but let me tell you of one example. During the Yom Kippur war in 1973 when the majority of Jews were observing a day of fasting and prayer Egypt and Syria decided that it would be an ideal time to launch a surprise attack. On the Golan Heights a patrol watching the border suddenly found themselves cut off by an invading column of Syrian tanks.

In trying to get back to their base and prepare to repel the invasion the soldiers found themselves in the middle of a minefield. They all got down on their knees and started probing the ground with their bayonets to locate mines and find a route through the minefield. It was already dark but they were unlikely to make it safely through before morning, but as they worked they prayed for deliverance when all of a sudden the sky went very dark, the moon was hidden by clouds and a strong wind sprang up.

The soldiers hunkered down against the wind while they waited for it to blow out so they could continue their work. Eventually the wind stopped completely, and the clouds cleared allowing bright moonlight to shine through and the soldiers stood up amazed. About two feet of topsoil had been completely removed exposing all the mines which were now totally uncovered. The soldiers were able to walk safely and quickly back to base.

Each of the wars against Israel have seen many such incidents, there have been five serious wars where Israel's neighbours have set out to eliminate the Jewish nation and every time Israel has prevailed despite being outnumbered and out gunned. According to military experts Israel should have been defeated every time. It should have been impossible for Israel to capture the Golan Heights but it did, and it should have been impossible to defeat the Jordanian troops stationed in Jerusalem since the Jordanian invasion of 1948, but it had been prophesied and it happened. It happened on the Jubilee or fiftieth anniversary of the Balfour Declaration in which Britain declared the area should again be the Jewish homeland, following the defeat of the Ottoman Turks.

Apostasy of the Earthmen

Hamas the controlling body in Gaza has fired thousands upon thousands of rockets, missiles, and mortars into Israel but remarkably hardly any Israelis have been harmed. Israel has spent a lot of money and effort to create air raid shelters and installed a system called "Iron Dome" that manages to destroy many of the incoming rockets. The work has been quite successful but it is not the only thing protecting Israel, a reporter when talking to a Hamas fighter about the rockets suggested they were not very effective to which the Hamas member replied, "Their God protects them." The reporter went to Israel and was talking to an operator of the Iron Dome system and suggested it was pretty effective and was told, "It is but we have some luck too. Some rockets were fired recently, and Iron Dome took one out but one got through but just as we were sounding the alarm the wind sprang up and blew it out to sea and nobody was hurt. It was a miracle."

During the Obama administration in the USA, a number of times the United States moved against Israel in support of various Muslim states and each time that happened a natural disaster struck the United States. There were floods, hurricanes, tornadoes, earthquakes and even a major oil spill from an oil well in the Gulf that can be aligned with a corresponding move against Israel. If you create a disaster a disaster will befall you, particularly when you act against the Holy Land. There are a number of videos and lists published by religious websites commenting on these phenomena.

Apostasy of the Earthmen

You might also have noticed that lately China has been suffering a lot of problems with natural disasters. This is not because of any serious action against Israel but flooding has become a major problem. This is China's karma for their actions in damming the Mekong River and causing drought in Cambodia, Laos, and Vietnam. In stealing the water from these people, the Chinese Communist Party has committed a grievous sin. China has also purchased huge water rights in Australia and is causing severe water problems for Australian farmers, even if governments will not act to stop this crime there will be an accounting.

Miracles and minor judgements are happening every day, but the inhabitants of the Earth have become so apostate that they are blind to the works of the Creator. Recently photos taken on the Israel, Syria border went viral on the internet, the soldiers on the Israeli side were working in bright sunlight while the Syrian side was enveloped in a severe sandstorm that stayed on that side of the border, the line of the border was delineated by the edge of the sandstorm. Denying the Almighty does not cause him to cease to exist, but it does blind people to the events around them that would otherwise alert them to their error. The misdeeds are compounding at an alarming rate and many are aware that the world cannot continue on its present course for very much longer.

We are in the twilight of the sixth millennium, the current Pope is predicted to be the last Pope and many other prophecies have been fulfilled pointing to the approach of the final battle, between good and evil. Despite the proximity of the conclusion we will not see a long drawn out series of events giving us plenty of warning. The Bible tells us it will come suddenly as a flood, most will be overwhelmed before they even know what is happening. This may well be a kindness as those who are facing harsh judgement will not have to spend many months worrying about their fate."

The group were silent and waiting to see if I was about to add anything further, but when I had not spoken for a minute one guest asked, "Do you really think this could all happen by next year?" I thought for a moment and then said, "We know that the signs are there that it will happen very soon, but only God knows what date he has in mind. We do know that the time is close, and I would expect to see some sort of sign around Passover, Easter for most of you. Then we could be fairly sure that the events will finalise before the Jewish New Year.

A war and an invasion of Israel can be expected because God said that he will assemble the nations in the Valley of Jehoshaphat and there he will contend with them for dividing his land among themselves and for their persecution of B'nai Israel. The invasion will be successful for a time and the "angel" or messenger from the East will arrive and Israel will be victorious over the invaders, not by force of arms but by the will of God. It might seem impossible in this modern age to imagine such a thing but just because we have denied it, we are unable to believe it could happen. The denial of the existence of intelligent design has created a blind spot that prevents us from seeing what is coming.

Some physicists and biblical scholars are the only ones who will be in any way prepared, and as the Bible warns it will be as in the days of Noah. People will be living their lives as normal as possible in spite of the calamities and economic catastrophe that is beginning to envelope the world, until the flood overtakes them, and it is too late. The only things I can do is urge you to do is study the Bible, give charity, repent any misdeeds and as far as possible to make restitution. The repentant will find forgiveness because we are all guilty of errors and sins but to repent and try to do better can lead to salvation."

Apostasy of the Earthmen

Chapter 26

This was as close as I had come to giving a sermon and I wondered how it had been received. It was now probably time to finish the series of talks as there should not be much more I could pass on in this manner, it would now take reading the Bible and giving explanations as I went through. I was optimistic that I might now have instilled sufficient interest that the group would now begin their own Bible study, whether through a Church or Synagogue or privately I had no idea, but I hoped for their sake they would take it on board.

The group were now seeing that there was a battle between good and evil, but it was not as they had ever imagined. I explained, "Instead of a cult like Satanic leader leading the world astray it is a quiet philosophy that insisted the history and culture of Judeo/Christian peoples was evil and exploitive. It has denigrated the forefathers of western civilisation and all but removed them from the knowledge of the younger generations. It has produced generations of ill-informed largely uneducated people who blindly follow the cultish groups determined to destroy all that which has made western society the most successful civilisation in history.

The science and achievement of the west in solving so many problems. In developing machinery and technology that have empowered the world, and medical science that has eliminated many diseases is downplayed as a new parasitic culture has emerged. Ignoring the patents and developments and stealing information to build a new culture that plans to replace the west with an autocratic atheistic, communist society. The socialist paradigm that has been built into the education system means that the younger generations have no idea that they are being manipulated and have fallen in with slogan chanting Marxist groups, without any idea what might be the end result.

Even when the Marxists who call themselves Antifa started burning Bibles in the heart of Portland USA, it did not raise any question as to the reason. The young have been taught to believe that this was a good and logical thing to do, and they have no idea where previous book burning groups have led their followers. History has already been rewritten by those against western freedom and democracy. The real truth is that their aim is the destruction of the religious principles that made western culture wealthy and powerful, for they have no interest in righteousness or justice, their sole aim is power.

This clash of cultures is not just a division into those on the left seeking socialism and those on the right seeking capitalism and free enterprise, it is a division into those who want freedom to follow religion and those who want the Bible and all it entails consigned to the scrap heap of history. It has become a battle between those who would follow God and those who wish to deny his existence and ban all references to Biblical teaching and law. The unfortunate part now is that the atheists far outnumber the religious, just as the Bible and the prophets foretold. The action against Israel and the Jews by all nations and led by the fervently anti-Israel United Nations.

On the very day that President Trump announced that the United States would recognise Jerusalem as Israel's capital and move their embassy to that city, the United Nations passed six different resolutions condemning the Jewish state. In the history of the United Nations they have issued thousands of resolutions condemning what they call "unjust actions" of these more than ninety percent have been directed against Israel. This is again proof of the accuracy of Biblical prophecy which warned that in the last days every hand would be against Israel. A particularly interesting prophecy because for two thousand years the nation of Israel did not exist. Except in the Bible and in the hearts and minds of the Jewish people.

All these prophecies and events serve to show that we are now truly in the end times and that the Biblical narrative is amazingly accurate. It is now time for the inhabitants of the world to decide, do they believe in God and are they prepared to follow the instructions in the Bible and pray for salvation. The other choice is to deny God, throw your lot in with the atheists and just hope that maybe this one prophecy is wrong, and two thirds of the Earth's population will not be destroyed."

Apostasy of the Earthmen

Apostasy of the Earthmen

Chapter 27

With this I had reached my conclusion and felt that any further discussion could not provide any new information, but with that I also knew that Bible study is a lifetime occupation. We cannot memorise the full import of those words in a single reading, there are layers to the Bible that we are only now just beginning to understand and some of these have been predicted in the very stories we read. In the book of Daniel, he is told to lock up the words until the time of the end and we are only now starting to fully unlock the hidden meanings. This implies again that we are now in the end times.

I addressed the group and said, "This is probably about all I can give you at this time but there is a custom that a Rabbi or teacher says a blessing for his students or congregation before sending them on their way and if you agree I would like to leave you with a blessing before we finish off today." There was some looking at each other and some nodding and then the atheist who started our little group said, "It can't do us any harm now that we have come this far."

It appeared that the once atheist group was now at least accepting of some possibility that religion might have some merit. I was not sure if they had actually become firm believers or just agnostic keeping an open mind one way or the other. I began with an explanation, "In Hebrew we refer to God's Holy Name as Hashem, which literally means the name. It is usually translated into

Apostasy of the Earthmen

English as THE LORD, all in capitals so that Bible students know when they see it that in Hebrew it was the name. The actual proper pronunciation was lost when the Ark of the Covenant was removed from the Temple during the invasion by Nebuchadnezzar about two and a half thousand years ago.

This is the name that some try to pronounce as Jehovah or Yahweh or similar variations. The letter Xet or Chet, which is a sort of guttural aitch that appears in God's name means that those pronunciations are not correct. We will not be able to ascertain the correct pronunciation until the Mashiach arrives and the spirit of the Lord descends on us all. Until that time, we are better off using the terms Hashem or the Lord or even Our Father, Our King.

I will recite the blessing in English for your benefit, but I will be using the term Hashem, so that the blessing is specific in asking God for his support. I raised my hands and said please bow your heads and close your eyes for just a minute, and I then recited the blessing. May Hashem bless you and safeguard you, may Hashem illuminate his countenance for you and be gracious to you. May Hashem turn his countenance to you and establish peace for you. May it be your will Hashem our God and the God of our forefathers that you have mercy on us and pardon us for all our errors, atone for us for all our iniquities, forgive us all our wilful sins and that you rebuild the Holy

Apostasy of the Earthmen

Temple speedily in our days, so that we may offer to You the continual offering that it may atone for us, as You have prescribed for us in your Torah, Amen."

I paused and the group all looked up I still could not be sure whether exposure to this idea had made any difference to the group but at least nobody appeared to be doubtful or agitated by the blessings. I then thanked them for their attention and explained. "I wanted to seek God's help and protection for the attention you have given my explanations and urge all of you to remember what I have said and where possible encourage others to learn about the Bible and history. To become kind, just, and merciful and good citizens, we need more people who do not wish to riot and destroy as a way of gaining what they want.

I have compiled all my talks into a book and hope that it will be published and released fairly shortly and if you leave me your email addresses, I will send details once the book is available. The blessing I have just extended to those of you here will also be extended to all those who read the book and especially to those who bring it to the attention of others and recommend the learning I have been encouraging all of you to undertake.

We can but hope to extend knowledge and encourage peace and understanding even though there are many who have no desire to believe or to have consideration for their fellow man. I mentioned earlier the real criteria by which we will be judged is by the way we have treated our fellow man. Those who have acted with kindness and mercy and given charity to help the less fortunate will be rewarded and saved, those who act with hatred in their hearts, or ignore the plight of others, will be judged accordingly.

May you all find salvation and acceptance in the eyes of the Almighty and may your good deeds be rewarded. Remember that it will all be good in the end, if it is not good it is not the end."

סיום

Siyyum

Finish

Apostasy of the Earthmen

Apostasy of the Earthmen

Apostasy of the Earthmen